Kenneth Lo's H...
Cook...

Kenneth Lo was born in Foochow, China, and was educated at the Universities of Peking, Cambridge and London. Since arriving in England in 1936 he has been a diplomat, publisher of Chinese prints, industrial relations officer (with Chinese seamen in Liverpool), lecturer, journalist, BBC broadcaster and professional tennis player.

But Kenneth Lo is best known today as one of the world's authorities on Chinese cooking. He has written many successful books on Chinese cookery; among the most popular is *Quick and Easy Chinese Cooking*, also published by Pan.

Apart from writing about Chinese food and managing one of London's top Chinese restaurants, Kenneth Lo now runs a very successful multi-region Chinese cookery school. During 1982–3 two television films were made of Kenneth Lo's activities: a six-part series by Thames Television on Chinese cooking *A Taste of China*, and a documentary film of his life by Central Independent Television.

However, the one activity that Kenneth Lo has pursued continuously throughout his life is tennis. He was Chinese Davis Cup and Wimbledon player in 1946, and more recently he has represented Great Britain in the Britannia Cup for Veterans and was selected to play again for Britain in the 1984 Crawford Cup in Helsinki. Kenneth Lo attributes much of his fitness throughout his very active life to his healthy Chinese diet.

ALSO BY KENNETH LO
IN PAN BOOKS

QUICK AND EASY
CHINESE COOKING

KENNETH LO'S HEALTHY CHINESE COOKING

PAN BOOKS, LONDON AND SYDNEY

First published 1984 by William Collins Sons & Co Ltd
This edition published 1985 by Pan Books Ltd,
Cavaye Place, London SW10 9PG

ISBN 0 330 28878 4

9 8 7 6 5 4 3 2 1

Printed and bound in Great Britain by
Richard Clay (The Chaucer Press) Ltd, Bungay, Suffolk

CONTENTS

FOREWORD

I started to write this on the morning of my 70th birthday. I went to bed the previous night just before midnight after watching the historic tennis match between Connors and Lendl which was transmitted live from Flushing Meadow, New York. The match was won by Connors. It was an incredible performance of fighting power, determination and unrelenting effort on the part of Connors; it was certainly one of the greatest tennis matches I have ever watched in half a century! I wondered to myself how capable he would still be when he arrives at the ripe age of 70 some nearly 40 years on? I believe that his capability then will depend largely on his eating habits for the next two score years. In the long run, other factors apart, man is still largely what he eats.

After waking up at 7 am, which is half an hour later than my normal waking hour, I indulged myself in doing 50 leisurely arm stretching movements, which have always helped in my awakening process. These movements are so easy and leisurely that they can be done even when one is only half awake. By the time the 50 movements have been completed I find myself completely awake, which makes getting up very much easier. At this point I get out of bed and carry on with my usual early morning callisthenics which consist of easy, largely circular movements (in the Chinese T'ai Chi tradition), which are all performed in a relaxed and easy manner, except for rising from a squatting position to an upright standing position. This I do 40 times divided into four series of ten. When I can do this with hardly any panting or effort, I know that I am in reasonable shape.

This is how I felt on the morning of my birthday and I

looked forward very much to playing in the National Final of the Men's Doubles Championship where the combined age of the pair should be at least 118. The event was due to take place in a fortnight. I reflected with some pride on my performance in New York last year in the Britannia Cup (the World Championships of the Over 65's) in which I had considerable success. I feel that I can do at least as well this year, but there is now the feeling that the legs and ankles are getting stiffer. This I believe can be remedied through individual care such as soaking the feet in hot water more often and giving them massage. I am looking forward more than ever to the next season of competitions. The outlook seems reasonably enjoyable and optimistic!

I recounted the foregoing mainly to put on record the mental and physical state of one who has just arrived at the threshold of three score years and ten, who has been eating reasonably balanced Chinese food all his life. By this I mean a balance between the meat dish with copious amounts of vegetables and in between some high fibre cereals. I admit that there is some room for improvement in my diet in the high fibre intake of cereals. The rice I have been eating in the past has been largely white milled rice – I should be eating more brown rice. I should perhaps be eating more fish than meat and also more uncooked vegetables (salads) than cooked. It is a question of a slight shift in emphasis, rather than the adoption of any new regime. To promote health, or just to remain healthy, there must be some discipline in the schedule of one's life. But I am not a believer in going at it one hundred per cent. What I believe is that for a short period of a few weeks one might go at it one hundred per cent, but in the long run one should adopt a liberal attitude to life and to oneself.

This I think applies as much to food as to anything else in life. I believe one should be able to eat whatever one is inclined to eat; to indulge oneself every now and then, but to bear in mind our requirements of proteins, minerals, vitamins and carbohydrates. In Chinese cooking, considerable emphasis is given to making all food as tasty and delicious as possible, while keeping it as fresh-tasting as ever. After all, foods which are appetizing are much more readily digested than foods which are unappetizing, however balanced and nutritious they may be. Hence in Chinese cooking and eating we tend to equate delicious food with healthy eating.

The enjoyment and appreciation of Chinese food

Throughout history, most Chinese have been hungry and underfed and therefore what they enjoy most is to fill their stomachs, mainly with rice, steamed buns and noodles. To add interest, these are served with small amounts of salted, pickled or dried foods such as salted or dried fish, salted peanuts, eggs or pickled vegetables, which are chopped up and sprinkled on top of the rice, or simply eaten together with the plain steamed buns or noodles. The joy and satisfaction of eating such simple food can be considerable. This is borne out by the fact that a Chinese labourer who is on the point of exhaustion after hours of exertion and physical effort can be miraculously revived, within a matter of seconds, after eating a couple of bowls of rice or noodles, accompanied by a minute amount of these spiced or salted foods, or a dash of soya sauce. I have witnessed this on numerous occasions, during the 1920s and 1930s, on long treks into the Fukien Mountains. The speed of the revival has to be seen to be believed! These spiced and salted foods, eaten together with soft rice or 'congee', still form the principal diet, together with preserved duck eggs, the famous 'two hundred year old eggs', salted and fermented bean-curd 'cheese' and dried ground meats, called the velveteen of meat or fish. The satisfaction which we Chinese derive from eating such simple foods lies in their warmth and piquancy, animated by the sensation of sharpness provided by the salted and spiced ingredients.

Once a Chinese improves his status, he demands a little more meat and savoury foods to go with the bulk food. At a normal meal, there will be a stir-fried dish or a long-cooked meat dish or a steamed fish dish. If there is only a small amount of meat available, say two or three ounces, it will be cut into shreds or thin slices and stir-fried with three to four times the amount of vegetables. The dish is further enhanced by the addition of a small amount of strongly flavoured ingredients such as garlic, onion or ginger.

These are stir-fried in the oil before the other ingredients are added, with a dash of soya sauce, salt, pepper, sugar as well as a few tablespoons of good stock which provides the sauce or gravy. If there is some meat from a long-cooked meat dish available, then this will be reheated and served with a vegetable dish.

For the more well-to-do, a long-cooked meat dish will be served, plus a soup. With such a combination the overall flavour of the meal will be much enhanced, and the diner will be able to enjoy the richness of the long-cooked dish with the freshness of the stir-fried dish.

In the enjoyment of the richness of a dish, the gravy or sauce derived from the long-cooked meat dishes are usually considered more richly satisfying than those made from the freshly made stir-fried dishes. To ladle the sauces and gravies into the rice and to eat them with small morsels of meats or vegetables is truly a great experience for any Chinese who is assailed with even a slight pang of hunger or simply a healthy appetite. Large quantities of vegetables are also eaten, having been made extremely palatable by the addition of a small amount of dried shrimps, good stock, meat gravy or soya sauce. The vegetable dish is more likely to be braised or stewed rather than stir-fried, as it is necessary to render it to a good degree of tenderness. When such vegetables are eaten in conjunction with rice they bring about an experience which is similar to the experience of eating long-cooked meat in gravy.

Watching the Chinese in their thousands tucking into food in the many cafés, dining rooms and restaurants up and down the country is a reassuring sight which reminds the onlooker like myself that the average Chinese is still capable of looking forward to (perhaps more than ever) and deriving some satisfaction from their daily existence. Because of the comparatively balanced diet the population is also healthy, indeed almost rudely so, compared with the other countries of the so-called Third World, in spite of the low basic material levels of their existence. Nowadays a good proportion of the people can expect to live to a ripe old age.

Looking at the reasonable health and longevity of the Chinese, the lessons we can learn from their simple diet and general approach to food can be summarized as follows:

1. Take trouble to make food delicious, so that it will be enjoyably consumed and therefore well digested.

2. Be sure that vegetables are not only lightly cooked but also eaten in quantity and that the bulk food (rice, buns, noodles, breads etc) is, wherever possible, fibre-rich.

3. Meat need not be eaten at every meal, although it can be eaten in quantity now and then. Usually, it need only be consumed in small quantities to act as a flavouring to less strong tasting bulk foods.

4. A light clear soup should be an integral part of every meal. It dilutes the spicier and greasier constituents of the meal, which then become easier to digest. A soup also provides the opportunity to introduce more vegetables if they are under-represented in the rest of the meal. Small amounts of vegetables, insufficient for a complete dish, can easily be added to a soup and served lightly cooked. On wintry days, drinking half a bowlful of steaming soup at the beginning and end of a meal has a comforting effect which is capable of throwing an altogether warmer, rosier and more consoling complexion over one's whole existence.

Bearing these points in mind, and from my own experience, I have found that the best way to compose and tackle a basic Chinese meal, which is quick, healthy and not too much trouble to produce, is to aim at cooking a three-dish meal to complement rice, noodles or any other bulk foods. These three dishes should consist of a soup, a meat/savoury dish and a vegetable dish. If the meat in the meat dish is limited and insubstantial, then its representation can be increased in the soup. The same applies to vegetables. In cases where there is an overall shortage of meats in the content of the meal, tou-fu (bean curd) can be added to the soup or the vegetable dish, so as to increase the overall protein element of the meal. It is all a matter of balance.

It should also be borne in mind that you should enjoy your food and therefore you need to make it as delicious and palatable as possible. Food is, after all, one of life's great enjoyments. So, to all readers and users of this book, may I wish you a lot of fun and good health with your Chinese cooking.

INTRODUCTION

Having lived now for over 70 years and eaten Chinese food all the time, I am still enjoying rude health and can therefore only conclude that Chinese food is reasonably healthy. Indeed, my feeling is that Chinese food and cooking can be extremely healthy if prepared and eaten with some regard for the principles of health and commonsense.

There are certain principles of good health which are inherent in the manner of preparing and cooking Chinese food. One is that you must always insist on the freshest of ingredients; this not only applies to meat (naturally even more so to fish and seafoods) but also to vegetables. Since we Chinese are great eaters of vegetables (the diet being 80 per cent or more vegetarian), being particular about the vegetables can make a great difference to one's total intake of food and its nutritive value. One very important reason why vegetables are eaten in greater quantity in the Chinese diet than in the average Western diet is that they are more deliciously and appealingly prepared. This is achieved in various ways: we make the vegetables more savoury by the addition of soya and meat flavour; more sumptuous by the addition of oil or fat (we do not have the same fear of fat, as we consume negligible amounts of milk, cream and other dairy products); and also by making the vegetables more appealing in texture and taste. This is done by placing greater emphasis on the freshness of the raw materials and in most cases cooking them for a very short time. Bearing all this in mind, it is not surprising that a large amount of vegetables are eaten at a Chinese meal – in the soup, on their own, with meat, as well as in conjunction with one another and with cereals and noodles. Because of the different ways of using vegetables in a Chinese meal, one does not notice just how many there are.

Meat does not feature as much in the average Chinese meal as in a Western one – nonetheless it still plays an important part in our diet. It provides part of the protein requirements, but somewhat inadequately because it is only eaten in small quantities. Luckily this deficiency is supplemented by various products of the soya bean, very high in protein, notably tou-fu (bean curd).

One of the most important functions of meat in Chinese cooking is to provide an element of savouriness in food. The Chinese frequently cook meat with soya sauce or other soya bean products and create some incomparable sauces and gravies, which when added to plain boiled rice or cereals make some very appetizing dishes.

Rice and cereals

Important as they are, meat and vegetables are not the central point of a Chinese meal. Rice or wheat cakes, buns or noodles take this rôle and provide the essential carbohydrates for energy. A Chinese does not feel that he has had a complete meal unless he has had quantities of rice; a person who is not an invalid would normally eat a bowl or two, while an adolescent or manual worker would think nothing of eating four or five bowls at one meal. The average man would feel that in the last resort he could exist on rice alone, however important meat and vegetables may be to make the meal more interesting and palatable. To live on meat and vegetables only would be a trial, however delicious they were, because they are considered, at best, only a supplement to the bulk foods of rice or other cereals.

Because of the quantity of rice eaten at every meal, some care should be given to its preparation if a meal is to be healthy. In the past in China, before the advent of machine

14

milling, the rice eaten was generally brown, which provided a certain amount of roughage and some vitamins. Milled white rice was at first only available to the better-off classes, while the peasants still lived largely on brown rice, sweet potatoes and other cereals. This partly explains the comparative healthiness of the Chinese peasants compared to that of the better-off classes who became progressively more unhealthy the more they ate!

When there is no brown rice available, the deficiency can be made good by preparing what we call 'Vegetable Rice', which is a quantity of vegetables (e.g. carrots, turnips, French beans or broad beans etc.) cut into sugar lump sized cubes and steamed in the rice. The harder vegetables are added at the beginning and the softer ones towards the end. A mixed rice and vegetable dish is often made more appetizing by the addition of a small amount of oil or butter when the vegetables are added to the rice. For the Chinese a dish of Vegetable Rice is suitable for eating on its own, sprinkled with a spoonful or two of soya sauce, and accompanied by a good hot bowl of soup.

Soup in a Chinese meal

Soups are perhaps more an integral part of a Chinese meal than a Western one. They are usually thin and clear and can be said to act as a lubricant to help wash down the quantities of rice and vegetables. In the case of richer and more elaborate meals with some fried or spicy dishes, soups act as an essential 'diluter' which takes the edge off any richness and considerably helps the digestive process.

Because of the important functions of soup, quite often there is more than one served at a meal. In a multi-course Chinese dinner, one soup is served after a rich and spicy dish and the other towards the end of the meal. When the flavours of the soups are well tuned, taking them at regular intervals during the meal, in conjunction with solid foods, becomes a very enjoyable process. It helps to break the monotony of eating often dry, solid foods throughout the whole meal; the drinking of a liquid, which is only lightly savoury but full of vegetable freshness is often a welcome change.

Some Chinese dishes are not quite 'full soups' but can perhaps be described as 'semi-soups'. This is where the liquid of soup in the dish only equals that of the vegetables and other ingredients. 'Semi-soups' can function in the same way as 'full soups'. Because of the amount of vegetables they contain they are usually welcomed when placed next to a large meat dish. It helps to achieve that balance and harmony which a Chinese meal, consciously or unconsciously, always strives to achieve. Since Chinese soups are mostly clear, and only lightly flavoured, they can easily be made from odds and ends of ingredients. The bones of spare-ribs, poultry bones, chicken feet and necks, ducks' feet, fish tails and fish heads make a good stock base which is made tastier by the addition of a small amount of dried shrimps, mushrooms and some chopped pickles and shredded ginger. When these have been simmered together for half an hour or an hour and strained, you have the consommés which are the basis of all kinds of Chinese soups. The other ingredients which only need to be lightly cooked, such as bean curd in cubes, soft vegetables or spring onions and herbs, need only be added at the last moment, perhaps only a minute or two before the soup is served. When there is the prospect of a good array of dishes for the whole meal, then the soup should be kept deliberately light, clear, uncluttered and somewhat under-flavoured. If there are only a few meat dishes the savouriness of the soup may then be increased by the addition of more shrimps, chopped dried mushrooms or shredded meats such as ham or bacon or sliced fish, seafoods or mushrooms. When these have been added and simmered for up to half an hour they should greatly enhance the flavour of the whole soup.

Speed in Chinese cooking

The majority of people who are interested in Chinese cooking are aware of the speed with which a dish can be prepared by 'quick stir-frying'. This type of dish usually takes no more than two minutes to prepare and two minutes cooking over high heat. In fact with experienced cooks using a strong hot fire, the time can often be reduced by half again. Incredible as it may seem, this is what happens every day in tens of millions of Chinese households. On the other hand, the Chinese housewife is often quite indulgent with time since her life is far less rushed than that of the average Western housewife. Therefore she often uses the process of long, slow cooking, where tougher cuts of meat are simmered over a smouldering charcoal fire or slowly cooked in a covered dish, which is placed in a steamer or in a pan of simmering water. Many people prefer this method of cooking, because it renders inexpensive cuts of meat extremely tender and tasty. The lengthy cooking process allows time for flavours to blend, and a delicious sauce or gravy is also produced. Such sauces are a boon to all big rice eaters. Another of the great advantages is that most, if not all, slow-cooked meat dishes are suitable for re-heating; indeed many of them are often improved through re-heating, with the addition of some wine and freshly chopped herbs, which only takes a moment or two. The majority of Chinese housewives will keep one or two of these long-cooked dishes in the refrigerator or pantry where they are available at a moment's notice. Because the majority of these long-cooked dishes are cooked in soya sauce (called 'red cooking') with wine and strong-tasting vegetables added, they usually keep well for several days in a refrigerator.

The provision of good stock is also an essential and integral part of quick cooking in China. Apart from its use in making soup, stock is extensively used in making sauces and stir-frying. When stir-fried ingredients begin to turn brown, or are even on the point of scorching, a couple of large spoonfuls

17

of good stock are often added to the pan to relieve the situation. A spoonful of wine or sherry may be added at the same time, along with a teaspoon of sesame oil and additional soya sauce, which when stirred or tossed together will result in an instant sauce or gravy. This can then be used straight away or slightly thickened by the addition of a couple of teaspoons of cornflour blended in water. All this compounding and stirring over high heat gives the Chinese cook a great deal of pleasure – he feels as if he is shaking up a savoury cocktail and that the ingredients can be varied according to his decision. Every 'cocktail' is his or her personal creation.

It seems that basically there are only two types of Chinese cooking, the long and the short. The most time-saving and economical way of preparing food is by stir-frying which requires no more than two to three minutes' cooking (unless using large quantities).

Long cooking in Chinese cuisine is represented by stewing in soya sauce, or 'red cooking', or Chinese pot roasting, where less soya sauce is used. There is also 'slow simmering' where meat or poultry is cooked slowly in simmering water for 1½–2 hours, and 'slow double cooking' where the food materials are placed in a covered dish and cooked either in a steamer or stood in a pan of simmering water. Using these methods, the food is usually cooked in a whole piece and cut into small bite-sized pieces just before serving. Consequently, although the cooking time may be lengthy using these methods, the actual preparation time is usually less than that taken for stir-frying. In short, contrary to the popular conception that Chinese cooking takes an enormous amount of time and labour, the truth is that although it may require a fair amount of work to prepare a meal, the rest can all be done quite quickly and easily.

The importance of vegetables

What has impressed the West about the Chinese treatment of vegetables is the speed with which we cook vegetables by stir-frying. It is a process not unlike making salads, except that we cook vegetables by tossing them in hot flavoured oil and in the West they are dressed in cold flavoured oil. In China the oil is flavoured by frying some strong tasting ingredient in it first, such as crushed garlic, shredded ginger and/or chopped onion or spring onion shavings. Then a good stock and soya sauce are added in the middle of the cooking, and finally a small amount of oil or fat, wine and sesame oil is added towards the end of cooking.

Vegetables cooked in the Chinese style can also bring a degree of 'freshness' to a dish. For instance, a large amount of Chinese cabbage or celery may be added to a long-simmered dish ten to fifteen minutes before the dish is served. This addition of fresh vegetables to a rich meaty dish, often helps to heighten the quality of the dish.

The sprinkling of a cooked dish, especially of the rice and pasta variety, with chopped fresh vegetables and herbs, such as watercress, chives, parsley or even shredded, diced young carrots or radishes, can also add a new element to such dishes – a vegetable taste and freshness which it would often otherwise lack.

In the cooking of a dish of mixed vegetables, the invariable rule is to cook the harder vegetables first, either by stir-frying or simmering in stock, to be followed by the other vegetables in reverse order of tenderness. Vegetables such as bean sprouts, spinach, tomatoes and cucumber are usually added last as they seldom need much more than one or two minutes of cooking over high heat. Vegetables such as mushrooms, celery, mange-tout peas and young courgettes should be added a couple of minutes before this, while the harder vegetables such as beans, cauliflower, carrots, aubergine, bamboo shoots, cabbage, radish and asparagus should be given a few minutes longer. As a rule in Chinese cooking, the dried and soaked vegetables together with the salted vegetables are put in first to fry in a small amount of oil, providing the initial flavour which eventually mingles with the stock. This initial flavouring is often reinforced by adding some dried shrimps and shredded salted meats with the salted and dried vegetables. It is this multi-stage flavouring and cooking which give Chinese vegetables that rich succulence so much appreciated by some of the top French chefs who have recently been visiting China. Indeed, one of them remarked that it was on a visit to China that he realized he knew nothing about vegetable cookery!

CHINESE COOKING METHODS

Quick stir-frying

This is the form of cooking which most Westerners associate with Chinese foods. It is the most popular form of cooking in China, partly because of its speed and partly because it is a handy way of treating food, which when cut into shreds, thin slices or small cubes can be readily blended together in different proportions, creating a great variety of dishes.

The usual way to stir-fry is to heat a small amount of oil (two to three tablespoons for a dish for two to three portions) in a frying pan or wok. You add the oil or fat only when the pan is hot (this helps to prevent foods subsequently added from sticking to the pan). When the oil is hot, add a small amount of chopped or sliced strong tasting ingredients such as onion, garlic or ginger to the pan and stir for 10–15 seconds to flavour and season the oil. Next add the main ingredients and stir them quickly in the pan which will now be very hot. The cooking time depends partly on the amount of the food and partly on the heat of the pan. The food required for two to three portions should require no more than one and a half to two minutes if the heat is sustained and the contents of the pan are stirred constantly. The food is then pushed to one side of the pan, away from the centre of the heat, and the remaining ingredients, soya sauce, stock, wine, sugar etc., are added. These are stirred and blended together to make a bubbling sauce which thickens quickly as the liquid reduces. The principal foods are then brought quickly back

21

into the centre of the pan, to mix thoroughly and take on a hot coating of the sauce. Within less than a minute the finished dish should be ready to serve piping hot.

This is a very general description of how quick stir-frying is normally done in a Chinese domestic kitchen. In a restaurant, where a great deal more oil or fat is used in the cooking, and therefore it is less healthy, the principal materials are generally deep-fried for a short time in an ample quantity of oil, then removed and drained of oil and added to another pan where the sauce and subsidiary materials have been prepared for the final blending and tossing together. This practice is not recommended for domestic and health-conscious cooking, mainly because of the quantity of oil involved, but also because of the need to use more than one pan.

Quick stir-frying in stock. This is a novel process which in the old Chinese culinary tradition is called 'Tan Po'. It should be of particular interest to people who prefer not to use oil or fat, although in Chinese stir-frying only a very limited amount of oil is used. In this case instead of using oil to fry, stock or even water is substituted, using about twice the amount as you would of oil. For instance, if you would normally use three tablespoons of oil for stir-frying an average three portion dish, if you substitute stock or water then you need six to seven tablespoons. The stock is brought to a rapid boil over high heat, when as usual the strong tasting ingredients are added together with salt. Stir these around for a few seconds so that the stock becomes highly seasoned. At this point the main ingredients of the dish, which should have been marinated beforehand, are added in small pieces. During the period of marinating, about one quarter of the oil normally used in the cooking is rubbed into the food. Because stock does not reach such high temperatures as oil, the stir-frying should be continued for about twice as long. The main ingredients are then removed and put aside as soon as they are three-quarters cooked. In preparing the sauce and the remaining ingredients you should repeat the process for stir-frying in oil, adding only a quarter of the oil normally used, and cooking and stirring over a high heat. Because of the high temperature which must be maintained, the liquid in the pan will reduce rapidly. As soon as the liquid has reduced by 50 per cent or more, the main ingredients are returned to the pan for a short period of mixing and tossing together. The dish is then ready to serve.

Steaming

Steaming is a very popular method of cooking in China; it is probably used much more often in a Chinese kitchen than in a Western one. This is due to the fact that a large quantity of steam is in any case generated in a Chinese kitchen because of the cooking of a large amount of rice; especially soft rice or 'congee' which needs four to five times more water to cook and takes much longer. Perforated metal trays or basketwork steamers are placed on top of the rice cooker, so that the food is cooked by steaming while the rice is cooking. This is one way of saving time and fuel in cooking since everything is cooked at the same time. Dishes which require most cooking should be placed on the bottom 'floor' of the steamer, and those which require least cooking should be placed nearest the top. In all cases (except when cooking soft rice when greater quantities of water are needed), rice cooked in conjunction with one or two steamed dishes needs at least 50 per cent more water added to the pan from the beginning in order that the boiling can proceed at full blast for at least 12–13 minutes before the heat is reduced or turned off. This generates a sufficient volume of heat to cook the top dishes. It is probably best to cook various dishes on top of the rice cooker only when brown rice is cooked, since it needs twice the amount of water than white rice, and must be boiled for 20 minutes.

Fast steaming. What I have described above is fast steaming. This presumes that the food or foods can be cooked in no more than 20 minutes. Although this is not a long time, a host of foods can be cooked in this way, including practically all fish and seafoods, most vegetables and some meat and poultry, especially when sliced or cubed. The cooking process need only take two or three times as long as stir-frying. A longer time is required only when cooking whole, thick fish, thicker cuts of meat, or meat on the bone such as spare ribs. In such cases the cooking time might have to be as long as 20 minutes.

One should bear in mind that in fast steaming, as in stir-frying, one of the principles involved is that the food should be cooked rapidly in order that it should retain most of the fresh juices instead of allowing the juices to be cooked out of the food. Here 'freshness' is an integral part of the flavour. Most of the flavouring agents used in Chinese cooking are in reality meant to act as a foil, in order to provide the essential contrast which will bring out and accentuate the 'freshness' of the food concerned rather than improve its natural flavour. Therefore only the best quality and freshest foods should be used for fast steaming. In these cases it is often the fact that the shorter the cooking, the more tender the food. Prime quality foods should in themselves possess plenty of appealing 'natural flavour' and so require no further manipulation and additional flavouring. Hence the fact that steaming is one of the best ways of treating fresh foods in prime condition.

Slow steaming. Cheaper cuts of meat require much longer cooking to tenderize them, and this prolonged cooking has at least two advantages: first, it is possible to develop a tremendous flavour and secondly, once the food has been cooked, it can easily be reheated and served whenever required. In other words, because such foods can usually be kept for several days, when prepared in quantity, they are a great time saver in the long run.

In Chinese slow-steaming the food is placed in a covered dish and steamed slowly for a long period of time. Because the dish is covered, there is no direct action of steam on the food, which over a long period of cooking would make the food too watery. This method is very similar to the Western way of cooking a steamed pudding. The advantage of steaming in this way is that as long as you keep the boiling water constantly replenished, the food will never burn and the cooking can continue as long as you wish. Usually in China the cooking will go on for hours or even overnight, and in some cases for several days. The aim is to produce tender, richly-flavoured food. Since at a Chinese meal several dishes are always served at the same time, a long-cooked dish is best eaten with the freshest foods which have only been lightly cooked (if cooked at all), in addition to the rice or noodles. It is not infrequent that when cooking long-cooked, steamed dishes, especially poultry, some fresh vegetables are added to the simmering sauce during the last few minutes before serving. This helps not only to freshen the flavour but also to improve the colour of the dish.

Braising

Braising in Chinese cooking is usually a derivative of stir-fry cooking. When foods have been stir-fried for a few minutes and it is felt that more cooking is required to tenderize them, or to render them more palatable, stock or water is often added so that the cooking can continue without the food burning. This method is often applied to the tougher vegetables rather than to meats. If meats that have been stir-fried for a few minutes are still tough or have become tougher, they are immediately subjected to much longer cooking. In similar circumstances vegetables only require slightly longer cooking, say up to 10–12 minutes. The addition of stock or water calls for some slight adjustments in the seasoning and flavouring, and not infrequently some thickening towards the concluding stages. These adjustments result in a slight change in the nature of the cooking from stir-frying to braising (or sautéing). Although meat often becomes tougher after the first few minutes of cooking, when used in conjunction with three to four times its own weight of vegetables, this toughening is less crucial in determining the eventual character of the dish when the meat is thinly sliced or shredded. On the other hand, the vegetables will have become much softer and more tender than the meat after this longer cooking. The flavour of the dish is enhanced by the presence of the meat and added flavouring and seasoning. 'White-cooked cabbage', cooked in stock, and 'red-cooked cabbage' with soya sauce, are typical of dishes which are produced by short braising. These are the staple Chinese domestic dishes which are extremely appetizing because they combine succulence and superb flavour. As a result, a larger amount of vegetables is often eaten than in most meals.

Barbecue roasting

Barbecue roasting is a method of Chinese cooking which can be used conveniently in the average domestic kitchen, since the cooking is done in an oven, which is standard equipment in a Western kitchen. The method is simple: the meat is marinated thoroughly, then cooked at a very high temperature for a comparatively short period of time, of say 15–25 minutes. When cooked, the meat is cut into thick strips along the grain, revealing the tender flesh inside, contrasting with the dark outer surface which is encrusted with the slightly burnt marinade. This contrast of a high spiciness on the outside with the sweet freshness of the meat inside is most appealing.

When poultry is cooked in this manner, because of the thickness of some parts of the bird, the cooking time may need to be a little longer, say 30–35 minutes. When served, the flesh is taken off the bone, or the bones are chopped through into large bite-sized pieces. If another couple of dishes are being prepared for the meal on top of the cooker, whether they are stir-fried, steamed or a soup, it is useful to prepare a barbecue-roasted dish because it leaves more room and time for the preparation and cooking of the other dishes.

Slow simmering

Slow simmering is the slow cooking of meat in water or clear stock in a heavy pot or pan over a long period of time. It differs from boiling in that as soon as the contents are brought to a boil, the heat is reduced to a minimum, and the liquid is maintained at a slow simmer for up to an hour, or several hours. Meats cooked in this way become very tender, and they are usually served with a variety of dips which help to make the food enticing. Because such dishes can either be eaten cold or reheated they are time-savers for busy people who only occasionally have time to spare to prepare food.

The ample soup or broth produced by slow simmering is also useful as an addition, in small quantities, to stir-fried dishes to prevent any likelihood of burning over the high heat, and to enhance the flavour of the dish. It is also good poured over hot noodles to make noodle soup.

Assembling

Assembling is the combination of various ingredients, some fresh, some cooked, with the liquid from a slow-simmered dish. They are combined and cooked together for a very short time, with the addition of some noodles (usually transparent pea-starch noodles). Such an assembly of shredded food materials, which often includes shredded, dried mushrooms and a wide variety of vegetables, all combined together in one dish under the 'blessing' of a neutral but highly savoury broth, can constitute a very nutritious and tasty accompaniment to the rice and other bulk foods.

Wet assembling (or 'hui' in Chinese). Wet assembling

indicates the tossing together of shredded ingredients as described above, and cooking them together for a short time using a good stock or savoury broth as the combining element.

Dry assembling (or 'pan' in Chinese). Dry assembly is the same process as above, whereby the ingredients are tossed together using flavoured oil as the combining agent (although a few spoonfuls of good stock may also be beneficially added). Frequently the oil used is derived from the cooking of 'red-cooked' meat dishes.

Red-cooking

Red-cooking is, in short, the stewing of meats in soya sauce. Only one or two tablespoons of soya sauce are added to about one pound of meat, so that it is not swimming in the sauce. Two or three times that amount of water or stock is often added to start with, but as the slow cooking proceeds the liquid is gradually reduced until towards the end there will be only a limited amount of 'gravy' left in the pot. It is best to red-cook in a heavy casserole with a tight fitting lid, so that the process of reduction will only proceed at a slow pace, and the meat will not burn. Water or stock may be added should the contents become too dry after half an hour. The resultant sauce or gravy from red-cooking can be considered the quintessence of Chinese cooking. It can be mixed or tossed with noodles or rice with a highly beneficial effect, or added to vegetables while cooking, which greatly improves the flavour of the resultant dish.

The main difference between red-cooking and stewing is that when red-cooking hardly any vegetables are added at the beginning, and only a limited amount of water or stock is added. The meat may be fried first before the liquid is added, but that is considered a refinement, as is the addition of sugar and wine during the latter stages of cooking. They may add something to the quality of the final dish, but are not essential. Because of the great richness of red-cooked dishes, they are best served and healthiest when eaten with plain cooked vegetables, or even salads, and quantities of rice and noodles.

Because red-cooked dishes usually keep well, and can be reheated as required, they are time-savers for busy people. They can be used first as a main meat dish or meat course, and later served as a subsidiary dish at other meals. For instance, on the first day a red-cooked dish might be served with a plain cooked vegetable dish and soup to be eaten with bulk foods. The second day it can be served as a smaller, subsidiary dish to a fish dish with a vegetable soup, or with a mixed shredded meat and vegetable dish.

Mongolian hot pot cooking

Hot pot cooking is the Chinese fondue where the cooking is done by the diners at the table, using plain water or stock to cook the food in. In the past the cooking pot on the table was heated with burning charcoal; nowadays it is more often heated by methylated spirit, bottled gas or electricity.

At a Chinese hot pot party, the table will be covered with one to two dozen dishes containing all shapes and varieties of food. If they need to be sliced, they must be sliced razor thin. When the liquid in the hot pot has been brought to a rolling boil, the diners start by picking up a chopstick full of thinly sliced meat which can be chicken, beef, lamb, pork, fish or seafood, and holding it under the boiling liquid for a matter of 20–60 seconds, when it should be well cooked. The food is then retrieved and dipped first in beaten egg, then a concocted sauce and then eaten. This is repeated perhaps a dozen times or more, or until all the meats, fish and seafoods have been eaten. By this time the stock in the hot pot will be well flavoured because of the amount of foods that have been cooked in it for a brief period. This gives the stock a freshness that can hardly be equalled in any other way. At this point several platefuls of vegetables, such as watercress, the heart of a Chinese cabbage, spinach, sliced mushrooms, and a bowlful of noodles are added to the boiling stock in the hot pot. A lid is placed over the pot to allow everything to come to the boil and to cook for just a couple of minutes before the lid is taken off and the diners allowed to help themselves to ladlefuls of vegetables and noodles which they transfer to their own bowls.

In the cold winters in North China, Mongolia and Manchuria, these bowlfuls of soup, noodles and vegetables are eaten in large mouthfuls to the great contentment and satisfaction of the diners. The benefit of hot pot cooking lies in the sheer freshness of all the foods eaten, their warming effect in the winter and all the fun and party spirit which both the cooking and eating are likely to generate.

MEAT

Pork is easily the most popular meat in China, and pig-keeping is common to all regions. To the Chinese, the bland flavour of pork, like chicken, is more acceptable than the stronger tasting meats such as beef and lamb. Pork can also be successfully combined with almost any other flavour whether mild, such as cauliflower, marrow or cabbage, or stronger. Beef and lamb, on the other hand, require strong, spicier flavourings such as garlic, ginger, chilli and mustard to complement them. However, beef and lamb are not eaten as much in China as in the West. They are most popular in North China (which adjoins Inner Mongolia) and the frontier regions, where cattle raising is more a way of life. In Central China and the South, animals and cattle are kept more as pets, or for haulage and ploughing, rather than for food. Hence beef appears on the Chinese table only once to every 10–12 dishes of pork or chicken. Both beef and lamb tend to toughen when cooked quickly, so only prime cuts of meat can be stir-fried or short-roasted whereas the cheaper cuts benefit from longer cooking, often producing very appetizing dishes. Indeed, because of the general limitation of house-keeping money in China, many Chinese home-cooked dishes belong in this category.

Minced meat and all offal are used extensively in China. Minced meat is usually pork, although now and then you also come across minced beef in Chinese recipes. Often this is made into meat balls, both large and small. The large ones are called 'Lions' Heads', which are usually fried first and then braised. At home, they are more often cooked as 'meat puddings' combined with vegetables in a heatproof bowl and cooked in a steaming basket over a pan of boiling rice.

MENU A

Stir-fried and braised minced meat
Sauté of mixed vegetables (carrots,
sprouts and mushrooms)
Boiled brown rice
China tea (jasmine, oolong or pu-er)

In preparing this menu, all three dishes can be cooked simul-
taneously. It might be best to start the rice first as it takes
longest to cook (unless it has been cooked previously). The
vegetables should be started next as they may take rather
more than 10 minutes. The meat can be cooked last as minced
meat should not take longer than 10 minutes to cook. First
of all, I will give you the basic recipes for boiled rice (brown
or white) which will be referred to later in the book.

Boiled brown rice

Preparation: 2 minutes   Cooking: 30 minutes

½ lb (225 g) brown rice – 2 oz
(50 g) per person

Preparation. Wash the rice under running water. Place it
in a heavy pan or small casserole. Add twice its own volume
of salted, cold water.

Cooking. Bring to the boil, then reduce the heat to a
simmer. Cover and cook for 20 minutes, then turn off the
heat. Keep covered and leave the rice to continue cooking in
its own heat for the next 10–12 minutes.

Boiled white rice

Preparation: 2 minutes   Cooking: 20 minutes

10 oz (275 g) rice – 2½ oz (65 g) per person

Preparation. Wash the rice under running water. Place it in a heavy pan or small casserole. Add 1¼ times its own volume of salted cold water.

Cooking. Bring to the boil, then reduce the heat to a simmer. Cover and cook for 8 minutes, then turn off the heat. Keep covered and leave the rice to continue cooking in its own heat for the next 10 minutes, when it should be flaky and ready to serve without straining.

Sauté of mixed vegetables

Preparation: 3 minutes   Cooking: 10 minutes

4 medium young carrots   **2 tablespoons vegetable oil**
¼ lb (100 g) Brussels sprouts   **1 chicken stock cube**
2 oz (50 g) button mushrooms   **1½ oz (40 g) butter**

Preparation. Scrape the carrots and cut into three sections and then into quarters, lengthwise. Remove any yellowing leaves from the sprouts and cut each sprout vertically into halves or quarters, depending on size. Cut each mushroom into halves or quarters and wash all the vegetables under running water.

Cooking. Heat the oil in a medium pan or casserole. Add the carrots, stir and turn them around a few times, then leave to cook over medium heat for 2 minutes. Add the sprouts and turn them with the carrots a few times, then leave to cook for a further 2 minutes. Add 4 fl oz (120 ml) water and sprinkle the contents with a crumbled stock cube. Allow to cook together for a further 2 minutes, then add the mushrooms and butter. Season with salt and pepper and stir the vegetables a few times. Bring to the boil, cover and cook over medium heat for 4–5 minutes.

Stir-fried and braised minced meat

Preparation: 2 minutes   Cooking: 10 minutes

2 medium onions
2–3 cloves garlic
2–3 tablespoons vegetable oil
¾ lb (350 g) minced beef
1 teaspoon salt
pepper

2 tablespoons soya sauce
6 fl oz (175 ml) water or stock
1 tablespoon cornflour
(blended with 3–4
tablespoons water)

Preparation. Cut the onions into slices. Coarsely chop the garlic.

Cooking. Heat the oil in a heavy pan or casserole. Add the onions and stir them in the oil. Leave to fry for 2 minutes. Stir in the minced beef. Add salt and pepper and leave to cook for another 2 minutes. Add the soya sauce, garlic and water or stock. Stir and bring to the boil. Cover tightly, reduce the heat and cook slowly for 5–6 minutes. Uncover and pour in the blended cornflour. Stir until the mixture thickens.

Serving. If the various dishes are cooked in casseroles they can be brought straight to the table for the diners to help themselves. The rice, vegetables and meat can be eaten from the same bowl or plate in the Chinese style, and served with a pot of China tea. Alternatively, serve a light soup. This might be a good idea if you have more than 4 people dining together, in which case the basic ingredients for the menu need only be increased by about 10 per cent to serve 5–6 people; the rice need hardly be increased at all, but a few extra carrots, sprouts and mushrooms can be added to the vegetable dish. All that is necessary to enlarge the meat dish is to add 1 tablespoon of soya sauce, 4 fl oz (120 ml) of water with 1 chicken stock cube, and an additional ½ tablespoon of cornflour blended with 2 tablespoons of water.

MENU B

FOR 5–6 PEOPLE

This menu is just an extension or enlargement of the previous menu. By making the meat and vegetable dishes somewhat larger it should be possible to cater for an additional 2–3 people.

These slightly enlarged dishes, because of the added ingredients, have a more sophisticated flavour. The kidney and liver give a new varying contrast of texture – these adjustments should please the most refined palate.

Minced meat dish

Preparation: 4 minutes   Cooking: 10 minutes

Add the following to the previous recipe:

2 lambs' kidneys	2 sprigs parsley and/or
¾ lb (350 g) calves' liver	2 sprigs coriander leaves
½ teaspoon salt	1 tablespoon soya sauce
2 teaspoons oil	1 tablespoon dry sherry
2 spring onions	

Preparation. Remove the gristle and membranes from the kidneys, then cut with a sharp knife into ¼ inch (5 mm) pieces. Slice the liver into similar sized pieces. Sprinkle and rub them with the salt and oil. Chop the spring onions, parsley and/or coriander into shavings.

Cooking. Follow the minced meat recipe in the previous menu, stirring in the kidney, liver, soya sauce and sherry to the pot or casserole 2–3 minutes before serving. Sprinkle the dish with the spring onion and herbs when serving.

Vegetable dish

2 oz (50 g) dried mushrooms
¼ medium cauliflower
1 oz (25 g) butter

Preparation. Soak the dried mushrooms in 5–6 table-spoons boiling water until soft (about 25 minutes). Break the cauliflower into even-sized florets.

Cooking. Add the cauliflower, butter and mushrooms (including the mushroom water) to the pan or casserole in which the vegetables are cooking for the last 5 minutes of cooking time.

MENU C

Steamed minced pork pudding with
pickles and cauliflower
Stir-fried spinach with garlic
Boiled brown rice (page 32)

Steamed minced pork pudding with pickles and cauliflower

Preparation: 10 minutes   Cooking: 40 minutes

Steamed 'meat pudding' is a frequently produced household dish in China, partly because it is a composite dish into which a variety of ingredients, mostly hard vegetables, can be added to cook with the minced meat, and partly because it can be left to stand and cook in half a pan of simmering water without having to keep an eye on it all the time. Although the time given for cooking the dish is 40 minutes, it can be left unattended, so the cook is free to do other things. Besides being a composite dish with vegetables already incorporated, it can constitute a whole meal when served with rice, so that you do not need to produce another dish if you are hard-pressed for materials or time. However, it is more appealing if served with another dish which is cooked differently.

2 medium onions
2 slices root ginger
¾–1 lb (350–450 g) minced
    pork
salt and pepper to taste
1 egg

1 tablespoon cornflour
3 small or medium carrots
¼ lb (100 g) cauliflower
    florets and chopped stalks
spring onion shavings

37

Preparation. Chop the onion coarsely and mince the ginger. Add to the minced pork in a mixing bowl and season with salt and pepper. Add the beaten egg and cornflour, stirring well to combine. Cut the carrots lengthwise into short sections and slice the cauliflower stalks to similar thickness. Pack the vegetables into the bottom of a large heatproof pot or basin and pack the minced meat mixture thickly on top of the vegetables. Cover the top of the basin tightly with kitchen foil, or greaseproof paper tied down firmly with string.

Cooking. Stand the basin in a pan of simmering water which comes halfway up its side. Simmer (topping up with boiling water when necessary) for 40 minutes when the dish will be ready to serve. Because of the flexibility of cooking time it does not matter if the dish is cooked 10 minutes longer or 5 minutes shorter. Sprinkle the top of the minced pork with spring onion shavings when serving.

Stir-fried spinach with garlic

Preparation: 3 minutes   Cooking: 3 minutes

1 lb (450 g) young spinach
3–4 cloves garlic
3–4 tablespoons vegetable oil
little soya sauce

2 tablespoons stock
large pinch of salt
1 oz (25 g) butter

Preparation. Discard any discoloured leaves and remove any tough stalks from the spinach. Roll up the spinach and cut through at 1½ inch (4 cm) intervals. Cut the garlic into thin slices.

Cooking. Heat the oil in a large saucepan. Add the garlic and spinach and stir-fry them by stirring and turning, over medium heat for 1½ minutes. Add the soya sauce, stock and salt and continue to stir-fry for another minute. Add the butter and when it melts turn the spinach over a few times and the dish is ready to serve.

Serving. When these two dishes are served together with brown rice they present an appealing contrast in colour: the dark green spinach with the pale brown pork, the cauliflower and orange carrots and the dark brown rice. There should be ample liquid in the bottom of the pork basin to moisten the rice. The texture and flavour of the stir-fried spinach will present a contrast to the tender contents of the long-steamed dish.

MENU D

FOR 5–6 PEOPLE

Steamed minced pork pudding with aubergine and turnips
Boiled vegetable rice
Marrow soup

Steamed minced pork pudding with aubergine and turnips

Repeat the previous recipe for Minced Pork Pudding substituting aubergine and turnips for the cauliflower and carrots. In this case use about ½ lb (225 g) of aubergine and the same of turnip. Cut the vegetables into 1½ inch (4 cm) triangular wedge pieces and pack them into the base of a heatproof pot or basin. Sprinkle them with 1 tablespoon of soya sauce before packing the minced pork on top. The minced pork should be prepared in the same way as in the previous recipe, adding 1 tablespoon of soya sauce to the mixture. Steam in the same way and for the same length of time.

This well seasoned dish is contrasted by the high vegetable content of the rice and soup dishes.

Boiled vegetable rice

Preparation: 4 minutes   Cooking: 20 minutes

1 lb (450 g) white long grain rice	2 rashers bacon
½ lb (225 g) Brussels sprouts	4 tablespoons water

Preparation. Boil the rice for 11 minutes in ample water and drain. Clean the sprouts and remove the tougher and discoloured leaves. Cut each sprout vertically in half. Remove the rind from the bacon and cut each rasher across the lean and fat into 8–10 strips.

Cooking. Spread the bacon and sprouts evenly in the bottom of a saucepan and sprinkle with water. Turn the heat on and put the parboiled rice on top of the vegetables and bacon. Bring to the boil, reduce the heat to low and leave to simmer gently for 5 minutes. Turn the heat off, cover tightly and leave the contents to cook in their own heat for 5–6 minutes.

Marrow soup

Preparation: 4 minutes   Cooking: 20 minutes

1 small marrow (about 1½–2 lbs (750 g–1 kg))
2 pints (1.2 litres) water or stock

1 tablespoon dried shrimps
1 chicken stock cube
salt and pepper to taste

Preparation. Peel the marrow and cut into large bite-sized pieces.

Cooking. Bring the water or stock to the boil in a saucepan. Add the marrow pieces, dried shrimps, crumbled stock cube and season with salt and pepper. When the contents come to a full boil, reduce the heat to low, cover and simmer for 15–20 minutes.

MENU E

FOR 4 PEOPLE

Spareribs and cucumber soup
Braised pork spareribs with onion and
pimento
Boiled white or brown rice (page 32)

Pork spareribs have become an extremely popular item of meat in recent years. In Chinese cooking they can be prepared and served in many different ways. To serve as an accompaniment to rice they should be chopped short, no more than 2 inches (5 cm) long. To serve them on their own to be eaten with the fingers, they can be cooked and served in the American 'Texan' way, which is in their full lengths. When buying pork spareribs it should be remembered that at least half the weight is bone and therefore twice the amount should be purchased compared with boneless meat.

Spareribs and cucumber soup

Preparation: 3 minutes   Cooking: 30 minutes

---

2 lbs (1 kg) pork spareribs
3 slices root ginger
1 medium cucumber

1½ chicken stock cubes
salt and pepper to taste
1 teaspoon sesame oil

Preparation. Cut spareribs into individual ribs. Chop each rib through the bone into approximately 2 inch (5 cm) discs, then into strips.

Cooking. Heat 2 pints (1.2 litres) water in a saucepan. Add the spareribs and ginger and bring to the boil. Boil for

42

5 minutes. Skim off the scum, reduce the heat to low and simmer gently for 25 minutes. Remove 80 per cent of the spareribs and put aside. Add the crumbled stock cubes and season with salt and pepper to taste. Stir and heat for 2–3 minutes. Add the cucumber, cook 2–3 minutes longer, then sprinkle with sesame oil and serve.

Braised spareribs with onion and pimento

Preparation: 5 minutes   Cooking: 50 minutes

3 medium onions
1 large sweet red pepper
   (pimento)
2 tablespoons vegetable oil
large pinch of salt
1¾–2 lbs (850 g–1 kg) pork
   spareribs

5 tablespoons soya sauce
2 tablespoons sugar
2 tablespoons hoisin sauce
   (optional)
½ pint (300 ml) stock or
   water

Preparation. Slice the onions and red pepper thinly. Prepare spareribs as in previous recipe.

Cooking. Heat the oil in a casserole. Add the onions, sprinkle with salt, then stir-fry for 2 minutes. Add the remaining ingredients and continue to stir and turn until all the contents are well mixed. Bring to a rolling boil, then reduce the heat and cook over medium heat for 20 minutes. Stir and turn the contents every 5 minutes. During this time the liquid in the casserole should be reduced by 80–90 per cent. Because of this the sauce should have become quite thick and very rich and brown with the soya sauce and caramelized sugar.

Serving. Because of the total cooking time of over 45 minutes, the meat on the spareribs will be easily detachable from the bones. This dish when eaten with rice and accompanied by the Spareribs and Cucumber Soup makes a highly satisfying meal.

MENU F

FOR 3–4 PEOPLE

In this case the recipes in the previous menu are adjusted to serve with noodles or spaghetti. The only adjustments which need to be made are the following:

Spareribs and cucumber soup

Add 2 teaspoons of dried shrimps which have been soaked in 4 fl oz (120 ml) of boiling water for 15 minutes. Both the shrimps and the shrimp water should be added to the saucepan at the same time as the spareribs. This addition should enrich the flavour of the soup.

Braised spareribs with onion and chilli

When frying the onions, add 2 shredded fresh chilli peppers and 2 shredded dried chilli peppers. The oil might also be increased by another tablespoon. About 1 tablespoon of salted black beans may also be added and the stir-frying increased by 1 minute. The stock or water should be increased by 40 per cent which will make more gravy available towards the end of the cooking.

Boiled noodles or spaghetti

1½ lbs (750 g) Chinese
   noodles or spaghetti
2–3 spring onions
1½ oz (40 g) butter

Preparation. Chinese noodles usually need no more than 5 minutes to boil and then can be drained. Spaghetti needs a bit longer, say 8–10 minutes boiling. Cut the spring onions into thin shavings.

Cooking. Turn the noodles into a large frying pan which has been greased with butter and stir over a low to medium heat for 2 minutes, or until heated through. Before serving, sprinkle the noodles or spaghetti with the spring onion shavings and 4–5 tablespoons of the gravy from the sparerib dish.

MENU G

FOR 3–4 PEOPLE

Long braised red-cooked pork
Stir-fried bean sprouts with garlic and
spring onions
Egg flower soup
Boiled brown or white rice (page 32)

Egg flower soup

Preparation: 1½ minutes   Cooking: 4 minutes

Egg Flower Soup is one of the simplest soups in the Chinese culinary repertoire. It can be 'knocked up' in a matter of 3–4 minutes and if served hot it can be quite satisfying when taken with rich-tasting dishes.

1 egg
2–3 spring onions
1½–2 pints (900 ml–1.2 litres)
  stock or water

1–2 chicken stock cubes
salt and pepper to taste
1 teaspoon sesame oil

Preparation. Beat the egg lightly in a bowl for 10–15 seconds. Cut the spring onions into shavings.

Cooking. Heat the stock or water in a saucepan. When it begins to boil add the crumbled stock cube(s) and season with salt and pepper. Add the beaten egg by pouring it in along the prongs of a fork and trailing the stream evenly over the surface of the soup. Pour the soup into a large bowl or tureen. Sprinkle the top with spring onion shavings and sesame oil. Put on the table for the diners to help themselves.

Stir-fried bean sprouts with garlic and spring onions

Preparation: 2 minutes   Cooking: 2½ minutes

2–3 spring onions
2 cloves garlic
¾–1 lb (350–450 g) bean
  sprouts
3 tablespoons vegetable oil

salt and pepper to taste
1 tablespoon soya sauce
1–1½ tablespoons sesame oil
  (optional)

Preparation. Cut the spring onions into shavings. Chop the garlic coarsely. Wash the bean sprouts under running water and drain thoroughly.

Cooking. Heat the oil in a large saucepan and add the garlic and half the salt. Stir a few times, then add all the bean sprouts and toss them in the hot oil for 1½ minutes. Sprinkle with the spring onions, remainder of the salt, soya sauce and sesame oil (if using) and serve.

Because of the quick plain cooking, bean sprouts are a good thing to serve with the following dish which is rich and long-cooked.

Long braised red-cooked pork

Preparation: 2–3 minutes   Cooking: 1¼ hours

1½ lb (750 g) belly of pork
2 slices root ginger
5 tablespoons soya sauce

5 tablespoons wine or sherry
1–1½ tablespoons sugar
10 tablespoons stock or water

Preparation. Heat oven to 190°C, 375°F, gas mark 5. Cut the pork through the skin, fat and lean, into 1½ × 3 inch (4 × 7.5 cm) pieces approximately. Plunge them into a pan of boiling water, boil vigorously for 7–8 minutes then drain.

Cooking. Transfer the drained pork to a casserole and add the remaining ingredients. Turn and mix together, bring to the boil and cook for 2 minutes. Transfer the casserole to the oven and cook for about 1¼ hours, stirring every 20–25 minutes.

Serving. Serve by bringing the casserole to the table. This dish together with the bean sprouts and soup should be eaten with rice. The melting, jelly-like quality of the pork skin is a great attraction to the connoisseur of Chinese food.

MENU H

Red-cooked pork with chestnuts
Steamed egg with shrimps
Boiled white or brown rice (page 32)

The previous menu can be varied slightly by adjusting the pork dish and soup. The soup can be changed into a dish of 'Steamed Egg', and chestnuts may be added to the pork when it is cooking. When eaten with rice it is recommended that the 3 dishes should be accompanied by a large pot of Chinese tea.

Steamed egg with shrimps

Preparation: 4 minutes   Cooking: 20 minutes

This dish is best prepared when cooking brown rice, as the longer cooking which the rice requires should generate sufficient heat to steam the egg dish on top.

2 eggs	25–30 shrimps (fresh, cooked
2 spring onions	or frozen)
1 stock cube	salt and pepper to taste
1 pint (600 ml) hot stock	2 tablespoons soya sauce

Preparation. Beat eggs lightly for 10 seconds. Cut the spring onions into shavings. Stir the crumbled stock cube into the stock. Beat in the egg and season with salt and pepper. Stir well and pour the mixture into a deep heatproof dish or basin.

Cooking. Place the dish in a steamer fitted on top of the

49

rice-cooker, to steam for 15 minutes. By that time the top of the egg mixture should have become firm. Carefully arrange the shrimps on top, then steam for a further 5 minutes.

Serving. Sprinkle the shrimps and the savoury egg custard with soya sauce and spring onion shavings.

Red-cooked pork with chestnuts

Preparation: 5 minutes   Cooking: 1¼ hours

Repeat the recipe in the previous menu. Add 10–12 chestnuts (shelled and with the membrane carefully removed) to the casserole when the pork is being transferred from the pan to begin its long braising. An additional tablespoon of soya sauce might also be added as the dish has been somewhat augmented.

MENU I

Stir-fried sweet and sour pork liver
Shredded ham with shredded Chinese
cabbage and transparent pea-starch
noodles
Boiled brown rice (page 32)

Stir-fried sweet and sour pork liver

Preparation: 5 minutes   Cooking: 5 minutes

---

1 lb (450 g) pigs' liver
salt and pepper to taste
1 tablespoon cornflour
1 egg white
1 red or green pepper
4 tablespoons oil

For the sauce
1½ oz (40 g) sugar
4 tablespoons wine vinegar
1½ tablespoons cornflour
  (blended with 6 tablespoons
  water)
6 tablespoons orange juice
6 tablespoons water

Preparation. Cut the liver into 2 × 3 inch (5 × 7.5 cm) thin slices. Rub with salt, pepper, cornflour and cover with the egg white. Cut the pepper into 12 pieces. Combine the ingredients for the sauce in a basin, stirring well.

Cooking. Heat the oil in a frying pan or wok. Add the liver pieces, spacing them out, and fry for 1½ minutes, turning once. Remove and put aside. Add the chopped pepper to the pan and stir-fry for 1 minute. Add the sauce mixture and stir until it thickens. Add the once-fried liver to the sauce, then stir it and turn over with the peppers for ¾ minute.

Shredded ham with shredded Chinese cabbage and transparent pea-starch noodles

Preparation: 5 minutes   Cooking: 7–8 minutes

3 oz (75 g) transparent pea-starch noodles
1–2 medium slices of ham
8–10 oz (225–275 g) Chinese cabbage

1 pint (600 ml) stock
1½–2 chicken stock cubes
salt and pepper to taste

Preparation. Soak the noodles in warm water for 10 minutes and drain. Cut the ham and cabbage into shreds.

Cooking. Heat the stock in a saucepan. Crumble the stock cubes into the stock and stir until dissolved. Add the cabbage, bring to the boil and cook for 5 minutes. Add salt and pepper to taste. Add half the shredded ham and all the noodles and stir into the other ingredients for 3 minutes, when the dish will be ready to serve.

Serving. Serve this 'semi-soup' dish in a large bowl or tureen, sprinkle with the remaining shredded ham.

This dish, which is quite a bulky one, should lend quite a lot of warmth to the meal when eaten together with the Sweet and Sour Pork Liver and Brown Rice; additionally each dish will contribute a good amount of nutritional value.

MENU J

Double-cooked pork
Sautéed cauliflower and courgettes
Boiled brown rice (page 32)

Double-cooked pork

Preparation: 5 minutes   Cooking: 28 minutes

1¼lb (500 g) lean belly of pork
2 medium onions
2 large red peppers
2 spring onions
4 tablespoons vegetable oil

For the sauce
2 tablespoons dry sherry
4 tablespoons stock

1 tablespoon cornflour
(blended with 4 tablespoons
water)
2 tablespoons yellow bean
sauce
1½ tablespoons sugar
1½ tablespoons soya sauce
1½ tablespoons hoisin sauce
(optional)
½ tablespoon chilli sauce

Preparation. Parboil the pork in 1 piece for 20 minutes, then drain. Cut the onions and red peppers into thin slices. Cut the spring onions slantwise into ½ inch (1 cm) sections. Mix the sauce ingredients in a bowl until well combined. When the pork is cool cut into 2 inch (5 cm) slices.

Cooking. Heat the oil in a saucepan. Add the onions and stir-fry for 2 minutes, then leave to cook for 1 minute. Add the pork and pepper and leave to cook for 2 minutes. Pour in the sauce mixture. Turn and stir the ingredients together over high heat for 2 minutes. Sprinkle with the sliced spring onion, stir and serve.

Sautéed cauliflower and courgettes

Preparation: 2 minutes   Cooking: 4–5 minutes

1 medium or large cauliflower
3–4 medium courgettes
2 tablespoons vegetable oil
1 oz (25 g) butter

10 tablespoons stock
1 tablespoon light soya sauce
1 chicken stock cube
salt and pepper to taste

Preparation. Break the cauliflower into individual florets. Cut the courgettes into ½ inch (1 cm) slices.

Cooking. Heat the oil in a saucepan. Add the cauliflower and stir for 1 minute. Add the courgettes and butter and stir for another minute. Add the stock, soya sauce, and crumbled stock cube. Turn and stir them together for 1 minute. Cover, reduce the heat to low and cook gently for 4–5 minutes.

Serving. If these two dishes are served with brown rice on a plate, put the vegetables and their liquid on top of the rice first, then place the pork and the rich sauce from the pork on top of the vegetables. The combined flavour of the two different dishes, one light and the other rich and meaty, should make the rice well-flavoured.

MENU K

Shredded pork in capital sauce
Summer vegetable ensemble
Brown rice with French beans

Shredded pork in capital sauce

Preparation: 5 minutes   Cooking: 4 minutes

1 lb (450 g) lean pork
1½ tablespoons cornflour
1 egg white
2 slices root ginger
4 tablespoons vegetable oil

For the sauce
3 tablespoons dark soya sauce
1½ tablespoons hoisin sauce
1 tablespoon sugar
2 tablespoons stock
1 tablespoon cornflour
(blended with 3 tablespoons
water)

Preparation. Cut the pork into thin slices, then pile the slices on top of each other and cut into shreds. Sprinkle the pork shreds with cornflour and rub it in, then dip into the egg white. Chop the ginger into coarse grains. Mix the soya sauce, yellow bean sauce, hoisin sauce, sugar and stock together until well blended.

Cooking. Heat the oil in a frying pan. Add the pork and turn and stir it in the oil over high heat for 2½ minutes. Remove and put aside. Add the ginger to the remaining oil in the pan. Stir a few times, then pour in the sauce mixture. Stir over high heat for ¼ minute, then add the cornflour mixture. Stir until the sauce thickens. Return the pork shreds to the pan and stir together for 1 minute over a medium heat.

Summer vegetable ensemble

Preparation: 5 minutes   Cooking: 7 minutes

4 tablespoons vegetable oil
2 tablespoons butter
6 asparagus spears
4–5 tablespoons mange-tout
  peas

4–5 tablespoons broccoli tops
4–5 tablespoons cubed
  aubergine
½ pint (300 ml) stock
salt and pepper to taste

Preparation and cooking. Heat the oil and butter in a saucepan or casserole. Add the vegetables and stir for 2 minutes. Add the stock and season. Cover and simmer over a low heat for 6 minutes. Serve in a tureen or bring to the table in the casserole.

Brown rice with French beans

Preparation: 3 minutes   Cooking: 28 minutes

1 lb (450 g) brown rice
½ lb (225 g) French beans
2 tablespoons vegetable oil

Preparation. Wash the brown rice. Top and tail the beans and cut in half.

Cooking. Put the rice in a saucepan with twice its own volume of water. Bring to the boil, reduce the heat and simmer gently for 20 minutes. Heat the oil in a small casserole. Add the beans, stir for 1 minute, then pile all the rice on top of the beans, levelling the top. Cover and simmer gently for 8 minutes.

MENU L

---

*Salt and pepper miniature crispy pork
chops
Bean curd with Chinese vegetable
ragoût
Brown rice with French beans (page 56)*

The pork dish in this menu is a dry, spicy dish. The sauce to eat with the rice is provided by the ragoût, which is full of vegetable flavour. Hot China tea would be a good supplement to all three dishes.

Salt and pepper miniature crispy pork chops

Preparation: 7 minutes   Cooking: 5 minutes

---

1 lb (450 g) pork chops
1 egg, beaten
4 tablespoons cornflour
2 slices root ginger
1 dried red pepper

1 fresh chilli pepper
½–1 pint (300–600 ml) oil for
  deep-frying
½ tablespoon sea salt
¾ teaspoon pepper

Preparation. Cut the chops into 1½ × ½ inch (4 × 1 cm) pieces. Blend the beaten egg with the cornflour, then coat the chops with the mixture. Chop the ginger and peppers finely.

Cooking. Heat the oil in a saucepan, frying pan or deep-fryer. It is hot enough when a crumb will sizzle when dropped in. Add the pork pieces, one by one, to the oil. Deep-fry for 2½ minutes. Remove and drain.

Heat 1 tablespoon oil in a pan or wok. Add the ginger, peppers, salt and pepper. Stir for ½ minute. Add the pork pieces and stir everything over high heat for ½ minute. Serve on a well-heated serving dish.

Bean curd with Chinese vegetable ragoût

Preparation: 5 minutes   Cooking: 30 minutes

4–5 medium tomatoes
2–3 medium courgettes
1 medium aubergine
2 medium onions
2 small sticks celery
1 cake bean curd

4 tablespoons vegetable oil
2 tablespoons light soya sauce
2 tablespoons hoisin sauce
(optional)
½ pint (300 ml) stock
1 chicken stock cube

Preparation. Cut all the vegetables into approximately 1 × 2 inch (2.5 × 5 cm) pieces. Cut the bean curd into 12 pieces.

Cooking. Heat the oil in a casserole. Add the onions and stir-fry for 1½ minutes. Add the remaining vegetables and turn them over high heat for 2 minutes. Add the sauces, pouring them evenly over the vegetables, then pour in stock and crumble in the stock cube. Bring to the boil, reduce the heat to low and simmer gently for 20 minutes. Add the bean curd pieces and turn them gently with the vegetables. Cook gently for another 5 minutes, when the dish will be ready to serve. Serve by bringing the casserole to the table.

MENU M

FOR 4 PEOPLE

Sliced beef in black bean sauce or
Stir-fried beef with spring onions and
shredded carrots
Vegetable rice with Brussels sprouts and
young carrots

Sliced beef in black bean sauce

Preparation: 4–5 minutes   Cooking: 4–5 minutes

---

1 tablespoon dried black beans
1 lb (450 g) beef (fillet, rump,
   topside)
1 teaspoon salt and pepper
1½ tablespoons cornflour
1 egg white

2 slices root ginger
1 medium onion
1 green or red pepper
3 tablespoons vegetable oil
1½ tablespoons soya sauce
3 tablespoons stock

Preparation. Soak the black beans in 3 times their own volume of cold water for 15 minutes. Cut the beef with a sharp knife into thin slices. Sprinkle and rub with salt, pepper, cornflour and wet with egg white. Shred the ginger and onion. Cut the pepper into ½ inch (1 cm) wide strips.

Cooking. Heat 2 tablespoons oil in a frying pan over high heat. Add the pieces of sliced steak, well spread out, and fry all over for 1 minute. Remove and set aside. Add the remaining oil, then stir-fry the ginger and onion for 45 seconds. Add the black beans and stir for 15 seconds. Add the soya sauce and stock. Stir until the mixture starts to boil. Return the beef to the pan and add peppers. Stir and turn them quickly in the hot bubbling sauce for 1 minute when the meat should be well-coated with sauce, hot and spicy and ready to serve.

Serving. This is an excellent dish to eat with rice or Vegetable Rice. If the following dish of lamb is served with it, and not as an alternative, the quantity of rice should be increased by half and there will be sufficient to feed 6 people.

Vegetable rice with Brussels sprouts and young carrots

Preparation: 5 minutes   Cooking: 30–40 minutes

3 to 4 medium young carrots
¼ lb (100 g) Brussels sprouts
1 lb (450 g) rice (brown or white)

2 tablespoons vegetable oil
1 tablespoon butter
1 teaspoon salt

Preparation. Cut the carrots slantwise into 1½ inch (4 cm) sections. Remove any discoloured leaves from the sprouts and cut each one vertically into halves or quarters (if large). Rinse and wash the rice under running water.

Cooking. Put the rice in a saucepan with 1¼ times its volume in water. Bring to the boil, reduce the heat, cover and simmer gently for 10 minutes. If brown rice is used, add double the amount of water and simmer for 20 minutes. Heat the oil and butter in a large saucepan. Add the carrots, sprinkle with salt, add the sprouts and stir-fry them for 1 minute. Remove from the heat.

Put the cooked rice on top of the vegetables in the saucepan and place over medium heat for 2 minutes. Turn off the heat, cover the pan and allow the vegetables and rice to continue cooking in the remaining heat for the next 10 minutes.

Serving. Stir the rice and vegetables together and serve in a casserole.

Stir-fried beef with spring onions and shredded carrots

Preparation: 15 minutes   Cooking: 4 minutes

1 lb (450 g) beef steak
1 teaspoon salt and pepper
3½ tablespoons vegetable oil
3 spring onions
2 young carrots

2 tablespoons soya sauce
2 tablespoons good stock
2 tablespoons dry sherry
1½ teaspoons sugar

Preparation. Cut the beef with sharp knife into large matchstick shreds. Rub them evenly with the salt, pepper and ½ tablespoon of the oil. Cut the spring onions into 2 inch (5 cm) pieces. Cut the carrots into similar sized pieces.

Cooking and serving. Heat the remaining oil in a frying pan. Add the carrots and stir-fry over high heat for 1½ minutes. Add the beef, spring onions, soya sauce, stock, sherry and sugar. Continue to stir-fry over high heat for 2 minutes and serve.

Mongolian lamb and beef hot pot

This is in effect the 'Chinese Fondue' which is an extremely healthy, complete meal in itself. It was first introduced from Mongolia into Peking in the 17th century and has now become one of the favourite features of the Peking (Beijin) culinary scene.

In Peking this 'fondue' consists of platefuls of very thinly sliced lamb which are placed on the table, then cooked by the diners themselves. After a dozen or more platefuls of meat have been cooked and eaten by the diners, the stock in the hot pot will have become very rich and savoury. At this point, noodles and sliced cabbage are added to the pot to cook for a short time in the boiling stock. After 1–2 minutes they are ladled into the diners' individual bowls, seasoned with the remaining dip sauces still left in the sauce dishes and drunk as the 'concluding soup'. Since without exception all the ingredients – meats and vegetables – are cooked only very briefly in the stock (mainly not more than 2–3 minutes) there is an unusual freshness about the soup.

Since few Western kitchens are equipped with a Mongolian hot pot, any heavy cooking pot can be substituted, or a large round casserole placed on top of a methylated spirit stove, calor-gas burner or an electric stove (or an electrically heated wok or chafing dish). Although unconventional they will all work; the main thing is to get the stock in the pan to come to a boil rapidly, so that when fresh foods have been added to the stock it will reboil quickly and be ready to take in the next batch of food.

In Peking the meat is hand-sliced into thin strips. Here in the West, I think it would be best to get the meat first cut by a butcher using his mechanical slicer, then further sliced at home into 1½ × 2 inch (4 × 5 cm) strips. This should greatly ease the preparation which is required for this dish. For an average hot pot dinner, one should calculate about ¾ lb (350 g) of meat per person; for the sake of variety the meat could be both beef and lamb in roughly equal proportions. When thinly sliced, ¼ lb (100 g) of meat should cover a medium-sized dish. Therefore if there are 6 people dining together it would be necessary to provide nearly 20 dishes of meat! They need not be placed on the table all at once; they can be brought in in phases from the kitchen, particularly as there would be other items to be placed on the table: bowls of dip sauces, bowls of vegetables, bowls of parboiled noodles. All these can in fact be very easily prepared and arranged. The initial stock to fill the hot pot can be lamb or beef bone stock, or one made from a chicken carcass. For an average hot pot about 2 pints (1.2 litres) is required, to be followed by half as much again for replenishment. In North China, in the countryside, often just water is used. The only items which require some attention are the dip sauces which have to be prepared and blended.

There are usually three types of dips that accompany Mongolian hot pot.

Soya, ginger, chilli and onion dip

6 tablespoons soya sauce
1 tablespoon finely chopped
   root ginger
1½ tablespoons chilli sauce
1½ tablespoons chopped
   spring onions

2 tablespoons stock
1 tablespoon vegetable oil
½ tablespoon sesame oil

Soya, mustard and hoisin dip

5 tablespoons soya sauce
2 tablespoons hoisin sauce
2½ tablespoons mustard
   powder (blended with 5
   tablespoons stock)

Soya and sesame dip

3 tablespoons light soya sauce
5 tablespoons sesame paste or
   peanut butter
1 tablespoon each vegetable
   and sesame oil

Blend together the ingredients for each dip sauce and serve them in 3 medium-sized rice bowls. These are passed round for the diners to take a teaspoon or two of each sauce to blend in their own personal dip bowls. In addition, each diner is provided with another bowl in which he or she will break an egg and beat it up lightly. Every mouthful of food retrieved from the boiling hot pot is usually first of all dipped in the beaten egg and then in the dip sauces before it is eaten. This procedure not only helps to give the food a good deal more flavour but also acts to reduce the temperature of the food quickly as it travels from the hot pot to the mouth.

When the dip sauces are prepared the meal can commence. The only other things which have to be provided are 2 large bowls of shredded Chinese cabbage (about 1 lb (450 g), 3 spring onions cut into 1 inch (2.5 cm) sections and 1 large bowl of noodles (about ¾ lb (350 g)) which have been parboiled for 3 minutes, cooled and drained. They should be added to the hot pot about 1 hour after the cooking has begun, so that they finish their cooking in the stock. To start with the only things to be dropped into the pot to get it started are a small handful of spring onions and a similar quantity of cabbage. Then a chopstickful of sliced meat is introduced and held under the surface of the boiling stock for often less than 1 minute, when it can be retrieved, dipped and eaten. Once the cooking has commenced, the slices of meat should be held in the boiling stock at an even pace until all the meat has been eaten. By this time the stock in the hot pot may require some replenishment.

The additional stock, the rest of the cabbage and the noodles may all be added together. These additions will lower the temperature of the stock considerably and it may take a few minutes for the contents to reboil. Let the stock boil for a further 3 minutes and then turn off the heat. A further couple of minutes should be allowed for the contents to cook and cool somewhat before they are ladled into the diners' individual bowls. Any final adjustment of seasoning may be made by using the left-over sauces in the sauce bowls. There are few soups that provide more satisfaction or a greater feeling of well-being than the last bit of soup of a Mongolian hot pot.

MENU N

FOR 4 PEOPLE

Cha siu barbecue quick-roast lamb (or pork or beef)
Hot-tossed salad
Boiled brown rice (page 32)

These dishes are best accompanied with cups of hot Chinese tea.

Cha siu barbecue quick-roast lamb (or pork or beef)

Preparation: 3–4 minutes   Cooking: 20–25 minutes
Marinating: 1 hour

1¼ lb (500 g) leg of lamb, or fillet of pork or beef

For the marinade
1½ tablespoons dark soya sauce
1½ tablespoons hoisin sauce
1 tablespoon yellow bean sauce
1 tablespoon mustard power

1½ tablespoons stock
1½ teaspoons sugar
1 tablespoon vegetable oil

For the gravy
8 tablespoons stock
1 tablespoon light soya sauce
½ chicken stock cube (optional)
½ tablespoon sesame oil

Preparation. Cut the lamb, pork or beef into 1½–2 inch (4–5 cm) thick long strips. Mix the ingredients for the marinade until well blended. Rub the mixture evenly and thoroughly over the meat. Leave to marinate at least 1 hour. Preheat oven to 200°C, 400°F, gas mark 6.

Cooking. Place the meat stretched out on a wire rack placed over a roasting tin. Roast in the oven for 20 minutes.

Serving. Remove the meat from the oven, when it will be encrusted with the marinade, but will still be quite rare underneath. Cut the meat across the strips into ¼ inch (5 mm) slices. Arrange them on a serving dish. Add the ingredients for the gravy to the roasting pan. Place over a medium heat and stir the mixture a few times after it has boiled. The 'gravy' is usually used in China to toss with the vegetables or rice to increase their flavour, rather than adding it to the meat, which seems to be the normal practice in the West.

Hot-tossed salad

Preparation: 3–4 minutes   Cooking: 2–3 minutes

3 sticks celery	3 tablespoons vegetable oil
1 cos lettuce	salt and pepper to taste
8 firm button mushrooms	gravy from previous recipe
2 medium tomatoes	3 tablespoons good stock
6 inch (15 cm) piece cucumber	½ tablespoon sesame oil

Preparation. Wash all the vegetables thoroughly. Cut the celery and lettuce slantwise into 3 inch (7.5 cm) sections, the mushrooms and tomatoes into quarters, and the cucumber into slices.

Cooking. Heat the vegetable oil in a large frying pan. Add the mushrooms and celery, sprinkle with salt and pepper and stir over medium heat for 1½ minutes. Add all the other vegetables. Sprinkle with salt and pepper, add the gravy from the previous recipe, and the stock. Stir and turn the ingredients around for 1 minute, then sprinkle with sesame oil.

Serving. Serve in a separate dish, or mix and toss the vegetables in with the brown rice and serve them together as rice and vegetable 'salad' which should be very appealing when eaten with the roast meat.

MENU O

---

*Long-steamed wine-cooked lamb with
ginger and turnips
Stir-fried shredded carrots, turnips,
bean sprouts and spring onions
Marrow soup with dried shrimps and
dried mushrooms*

Long-steamed wine-cooked lamb with ginger and turnips

Preparation: 5 minutes   Cooking: 2½–3 hours

The lamb may be substituted with beef, in which case the cooking time should be increased by 30 minutes.

1½ lb (750 g) leg of lamb (or chuck steak or braising beef)
½ lb (225 g) turnips
3 tablespoons vegetable oil
5 slices root ginger

¾ teaspoon salt
pepper to taste
4 tablespoons light soya sauce
3 teaspoons sugar
½ pint (300 ml) good stock
½ bottle red or white wine

Preparation. Cut the lamb into 1¼ inch (3 cm) cubes and the turnip into similar sized pieces.

Cooking. Heat the oil in a saucepan. Add the ginger and lamb and stir over high heat for 2 minutes. Sprinkle with salt and pepper, then continue to stir and turn for another 1½ minutes. Add the turnips, soya sauce, sugar and stock. Bring to the boil and simmer for 5 minutes. Turn the mixture into a round casserole and, if it is to be steamed in the Chinese

67

way, put the casserole into a very large saucepan filled with 2½ inches (6 cm) depth of water which should come about half the way up the sides of the casserole. Cook gently for 2½ hours, adding the wine during the last hour of cooking. Alternatively, place the casserole in a preheated oven at 180°C, 350°F, gas mark 4 for 2 hours, turning the contents over every 30 minutes. Add the wine during the last hour of cooking as before.

Serving. Lamb or beef cooked in this way is a very rich dish and should be eaten with quantities of rice or noodles and plenty of vegetables.

Stir-fried shredded carrots, turnips, bean sprouts and spring onions

Preparation: 5–6 minutes   Cooking: 6–7 minutes

4 medium carrots
5 oz (150 g) turnips
½ lb (225 g) bean sprouts
3 tablespoons vegetable oil
1 teaspoon salt

4 spring onions
1 tablespoon soya sauce
4 tablespoons sauce from the
  previous recipe

Preparation. Clean and cut carrots and turnips into double matchstick shreds. Parboil for 3 minutes in boiling water and drain. Rinse the bean sprouts under running water and pat dry.

Cooking. Heat the oil in a frying pan. Add the shredded carrots and turnips, sprinkle with salt and stir-fry over high heat for 2 minutes. Add the sprouts and spring onions, sprinkle with soya sauce and gravy, continue to turn and stir-fry for 2–3 minutes.

Serving. Serve with rice or noodles, together with beef or lamb.

Marrow soup with dried shrimps and dried mushrooms

Preparation: 28 minutes   Cooking: 15 minutes

1½ tablespoons Chinese dried
  shrimps
4–5 medium Chinese dried
  mushrooms
1½ lb (750 g) marrow
2 tablespoons vegetable oil

3 slices root ginger
1 chicken stock cube
salt and pepper to taste
1½ pints (1 litre) good stock
1 teaspoon sesame oil

Preparation. Soak the shrimps and mushrooms in a bowl of boiling water for 20 minutes. Remove the stem from the mushrooms and cut the caps into shreds. Retain the soaking water. Peel the marrow, cut in half and remove the seeds. Cut the marrow into bite-sized pieces then parboil in boiling water for 3 minutes and drain.

Cooking. Heat the vegetable oil in a saucepan. Add the shredded mushrooms and ginger and stir-fry for 1 minute. Add the remaining ingredients (except the sesame oil). Bring to the boil, reduce heat and simmer for 10 minutes when the soup will be ready to serve.

Serving. Sprinkle the soup with sesame oil and either pour into individual bowls or into a large tureen for the diners to ladle into their own bowls and drink. The high vegetable content of the soup gives it a delicious sweetness contrasting well with the mushrooms and shrimps.

MENU P

---

*Stir-fried lambs' kidneys with
mushrooms and celery or Jelly of lamb
Steamed French beans with bacon,
garlic and transparent pea-starch
noodles
Hot-tossed savoury rice with peas and
eggs*

Stir-fried lambs' kidneys with mushrooms and celery

Preparation: 10 minutes   Cooking: 5 minutes
Marinating: 10 minutes

5–6 lambs' kidneys	3 sticks celery
salt and pepper to taste	½ lb (225 g) button
1½ tablespoons soya sauce	mushrooms
2 teaspoons chilli sauce	3 tablespoons good stock
4 tablespoons vegetable oil	3 tablespoons dry sherry

Preparation. Remove the membrane and gristle from the kidneys. Wash and pat dry. Sprinkle and rub with salt, pepper, soya sauce, chilli sauce and 2 teaspoons of the oil. Leave to marinate for 10 minutes. Meanwhile, wash and cut celery slantwise into 1 inch (2.5 cm) sections. Prepare the mushrooms by removing the stalks and cutting them in half. Cut the caps in quarters.

Cooking. Heat the remaining oil in a frying pan. Add the kidney and stir-fry quickly for 1 minute over high heat, then remove and put aside. Add the vegetables and salt and pepper. Stir-fry over high heat for 1 minute. Add the stock and sherry and return the kidneys to the pan. Stir-fry together for 1½ minutes and serve.

Steamed French beans with bacon, garlic and transparent pea-starch noodles

---

Preparation: 5 minutes   Cooking: 20 minutes

---

1 lb (450 g) French beans
2–3 rashers bacon
3 cloves garlic
3½ oz (90 g) transparent pea-
  starch noodles

2 tablespoons vegetable oil
½ pint (300 ml) good stock
salt and pepper to taste
½ chicken stock cube

Preparation. Top and tail the French beans, then wash and drain them. Cut the bacon across lean and fat into shreds, having removed the rind. Cut the garlic into thin slices. Soak the noodles in a basin of hot water for 2 minutes and use scissors to cut them into 2–3 inch (5–7.5 cm) sections.

Cooking. Heat the oil in a saucepan. Add the bacon and garlic and stir-fry over medium heat for 1 minute. Add the beans and continue to stir-fry over high heat for 1½ minutes. Pour in the stock and season with salt and pepper. Bring to the boil, sprinkle with crumbled stock cube and add the noodles. Pour into a heatproof basin and steam for 10–15 minutes when the dish will be ready to serve.

Serving. Serve by bringing the basin to the table for the diners to help themselves. This is what we call in China a 'semi-soup' dish which is very warming and satisfying for accompanying rice or fried rice and stir-fried dishes.

Hot-tossed savoury rice with peas and eggs

Preparation: 2 minutes   Cooking: 4 minutes

4 eggs
2 spring onions
3½ tablespoons vegetable oil
¼ lb (100 g) peas (fresh or
   frozen)

1½ oz (40 g) butter
1¼ lb (500 g) cooked rice
   (white or brown)
1½ tablespoons light soya
   sauce

Preparation. Beat the eggs lightly in a bowl. Clean and cut the spring onions into shavings.

Cooking. Heat the oil in a frying-pan. Add the peas, stir and turn them over high heat for 1 minute, then push them to one side of the pan. Add the butter to the other side. When it has melted, pour the beaten eggs over it. Stir and scramble the eggs and, when they have set, add all the rice and soya sauce and stir with the peas and eggs. When heated through, turn onto a serving dish.

Serving. Sprinkle the eggs, peas and rice evenly with spring onion shavings and soya sauce and bring the dish to the table for the diners to help themselves.

Jelly of lamb (for 4–6 people)

Preparation: 10 minutes   Cooking: 1½ hours

In North China where lamb or mutton are plentiful and popular, this is another convenient dish which is frequently served with the hot-tossed rice and a semi-soup dish.

2½–3 lbs (1.25 kg) neck of
   lamb
2 oz (50 g) pork skin
3 slices root ginger
2½ teaspoons salt
pepper to taste

For later addition
2–3 sprigs parsley
2 spring onions
2 oz (50 g) aspic jelly
2 tablespoons dry sherry
1 tablespoon light soya sauce

Preparation and cooking. Parboil the neck of lamb in a

large saucepan of boiling water for 4–5 minutes, then drain. Place the lamb in a saucepan with 2 pints (1.2 litres) of water, together with the pork skin, ginger, salt and pepper. Bring to the boil, reduce the heat, cover and simmer gently for 1½ hours. Meanwhile, chop the parsley and cut the spring onions into 2 inch (5 cm) lengths and dissolve the jelly in 5–6 table-spoons warm water.

Setting. Remove the pork skin from the saucepan. Scrape and cut the lamb meat from the bones. Discard the bones. Cut the meat into regular sized pieces. Pour the cooking liquid into a basin and allow it to cool; skim away fat and impurities from the top. Stir in the meat, spring onions, parsley, sherry, soya sauce and dissolved jelly. Pour the contents of the basin into a saucepan and bring to a gentle boil. Stir the contents so that the solids in the soup are evenly distributed. Pour into a deep heat-proof glass dish or oblong mould. Leave to cool, then chill in the refrigerator for 2–3 hours, when the jelly should have set firmly.

Serving. Turn out the jelly on to a flat dish and cut into 6 blocks. When served with Hot-Tossed Savoury Rice a block of Jelly of Lamb should be placed on top of the rice, to allow the jelly to melt slowly into the hot rice. When served with a vegetable dish, such as Steamed French Beans, they make a substantial and appealing meal. The two remaining blocks of lamb should be further cut into halves for the hungrier diners to help themselves.

MENU Q

---

*Long-cooked soya-braised beef with
kidney and carrots
White-cooked cabbage
Plain-cooked noodles with shredded
cucumber and bean sprouts*

When these 3 dishes are served to be eaten together, diners should fill their individual bowls first with the noodles and cucumber and then add the cabbage, with the beef on top. Mouthfuls of noodles with cabbage and beef should be very satisfying to tuck into for anyone with an appetite.

Long-cooked soya-braised beef with kidney and carrots

Preparation: 5 minutes   Cooking: 1½ hours

1½ lb (750 g) stewing beef or
  chuck steak
3 medium carrots
2–3 calves' kidneys
3 slices root ginger
2½ tablespoons vegetable oil

1 teaspoon salt
3 tablespoons dark soya sauce
¾ pint (450 ml) good stock
3 tablespoons dry sherry
1 tablespoon sugar

Preparation. Preheat oven to 190°C, 375°F, gas mark 5. Cut the beef into large bite-sized pieces and the carrots slant-wise into 1 inch (2.5 cm) sections. Remove the membrane and gristle from the kidneys and make 6 criss-cross cuts halfway through the smooth surface of the kidneys, then cut each piece into quarters.

Cooking. Heat the oil in a medium casserole. Add the ginger and beef and stir-fry over high heat for 2 minutes. Add the kidneys and continue to stir-fry for 1 minute. Add the remaining ingredients and pour in the stock. Bring to the boil, stirring. Cover and cook in a preheated oven at 190°C, 375°F, gas mark 5 for 30 minutes. Reduce the heat to 180°C, 350°F, gas mark 4 and continue cooking for 1 hour, turning the contents over twice during cooking.

Serving. Bring the casserole to the table for the diners to help themselves. This is a rich dish and should be eaten with ample rice or noodles and plentiful vegetables.

White-cooked cabbage

Preparation: 3–4 minutes   Cooking: 17 minutes

In Chinese cooking, dishes cooked without the use of soya sauce are frequently called white-cooked.

1 medium Savoy cabbage	1½ tablespoons sugar
2 rashers bacon	1½ oz (40 g) butter
2 tablespoons vegetable oil	1 chicken stock cube
½ pint (300 ml) good stock	salt and pepper to taste

Preparation. Clean and cut the cabbage into 20 pieces, including one third of the tough stem. Cut the bacon across the lean and fat into double matchstick shreds, having removed the rind.

Cooking. Heat the oil in a saucepan. Add the bacon and stir-fry over medium heat for 2 minutes. Add the cabbage and the remaining ingredients. Bring the contents to the boil, stirring twice. Reduce the heat, cover and simmer gently for 15 minutes.

Serving. This is a light dish, with a sweet vegetable flavour.

It encourages the diner to eat quantities of vegetables and is an ideal complement to rich meat dishes.

Plain-cooked noodles with shredded cucumber and bean sprouts

Preparation: 5 minutes   Cooking: 6–10 minutes

---

8 inch (20 cm) piece of
  cucumber
2 spring onions
1 lb (450 g) Chinese noodles or
  spaghetti

2 tablespoons vegetable oil
1½ tablespoons butter
½ lb (225 g) bean sprouts
2 teaspoons sesame oil

Preparation. Cut the cucumber into double matchstick shreds and the spring onions into 1 inch (2.5 cm) sections. Heat the oil in a small pan. Add the butter to melt and blend with the oil.

Cooking and serving. Boil the noodles for 5–6 minutes, or the spaghetti for 8–10 minutes. Add the bean sprouts to boil together during the last 2 minutes. Drain well, and while still hot, pour over the oil-butter mixture and toss in the shredded cucumber and spring onion. Sprinkle with sesame oil. Turn and toss all the ingredients together and serve to be eaten together with the meat and vegetable dishes.

On occasions when there is a shortage and there is no meat available, 2–3 tablespoons of peanut butter may be stirred into the noodles to mix with the other ingredients to make it a much richer dish. In this case, the richer noodle dish, accompanied by just the vegetable dish should be sufficient to make a substantial and satisfying meal.

MENU R

FOR 4 PEOPLE

*Water 'fried' sliced beef with leeks
Hot-tossed noodle soup with shredded
carrots, celery and spring onions*

Water 'fried' sliced beef with leeks

Preparation: 5 minutes   Cooking: 5 minutes
Marinating: 30 minutes

Frying is, of course, normally done with oil, but it can also
be done with a controlled amount of water. If not too much
water is used and if it is kept consistently at a rolling boil,
it will simulate the effect of normal Chinese quick stir-frying.
The cooking time should not exceed 2–3 minutes.

1¼ lb (500 g) beef (fillet,
    rump, topside)
½ teaspoon salt and pepper
1 teaspoon sugar
2½ tablespoons dark soya
    sauce
1½ tablespoons vegetable oil

1½ tablespoons cornflour
1 egg white
½ lb (225 g) young leeks
¼ pint (150 ml) water or
    stock
1 tablespoon light soya sauce
½ tablespoon chilli sauce

Preparation. Cut the beef into very thin 1 × 1½ inch (2.5
× 4 cm) slices. Rub them thoroughly with salt, pepper,
sugar, dark soya sauce and oil. Leave to marinate for 30
minutes. Sprinkle and rub the beef evenly with the cornflour,
then wet with the egg white. Cut the leeks into 2 inch (5 cm)
pieces and then shred lengthwise.
Cooking. Heat the water or stock in a frying pan or wok
over high heat. When the water has come to a rolling boil,

add the leeks and spread them evenly in the pan. Sprinkle with light soya sauce and chilli sauce. Bring to the boil quickly and stir-fry for 1½ minutes. During this time about one-third of the water will have evaporated. Now add the beef, piece by piece, spreading it evenly over the leeks. Leave to cook in the steam and boiling stock for 45 seconds. Stir for a further 30–45 seconds.

Serving. Like other stir-fried dishes, this dish should be eaten hot and as soon as possible after it leaves the pan. Because of the ingredients which have been rubbed into the meat (including the oil) and the high heat at which it is being cooked, it should have a quality and flavour very similar to a dish which has been stir-fried in oil. For those who are particular about their intake of oil or fat, the fact that this beef has been cooked mainly in water should be an added attraction.

Hot-tossed noodle soup with shredded carrots, celery and spring onions

Preparation: 10–15 minutes   Cooking: 10 minutes

In Chinese food and cooking, noodles are frequently used as 'bulk food' to lend substance to a meal. When soup and vegetables are added at the same time and cooked together they can act both as a soup and as a vegetable dish. The following recipe is a typical example.

1¼ lb (500 g) Chinese noodles
  or spaghetti
3 medium young carrots
2 sticks celery
2 oz (50 g) ham
3 spring onions
1 chicken stock cube

1½ pints (900 ml) good stock
1½ inch (4 cm) piece gherkin
  (or Chinese 'snow pickle')
2 tablespoons light soya sauce
salt and pepper to taste
1½ teaspoons sesame oil

Preparation. Boil the noodles for 5 minutes or spaghetti for 8–10 minutes, then drain. Clean and cut the carrots and celery into double matchstick shreds. Cut the ham into similar sized shreds and the spring onions into 2 inch (5 cm) pieces. Dissolve the stock cube in the stock. Coarsely chop the gherkin or snow pickle.

Cooking. Toss the ham and shredded vegetables with the noodles in a large saucepan. Pour in the stock, add the soya sauce and bring to a gentle boil. Add salt and pepper, then simmer gently for 5 minutes. Sprinkle with sesame oil and chopped gherkin or pickles.

Serving. Divide the noodles and soup between 4–5 bowls and serve like Western soup. This is a dish which is eaten as well as drunk at the same time. The quantity cooked here is probably enough to fill 4 average bowls. Eaten together with the tasty beef and leeks these dishes complement each other well. Fortunately there should be some left in the pan for 'seconds'.

CHICKEN

In China, chicken and pork are considered to be similar, because they share the same rather neutral flavour. This makes it possible to combine chicken with a wide range of other ingredients to produce a variety of different dishes. Because the flavour is light compared to other gamier meats, chicken combines particularly successfully with ingredients which have a more subtle flavour, such as mushrooms, Chinese cabbage or lettuce, cauliflower etc. These light, subtle-flavoured vegetables would be swamped by the flavour of gamier meats, which need to be cooked with stronger tasting vegetables.

Because of the light flavour of chicken, the stock made from prolonged boiling of a chicken or chicken carcass can be used to add flavour to vegetables, pasta or mixed ingredient dishes without completely camouflaging them. Perhaps for this reason, one of the most common and popular ways of cooking chicken is to boil it so that a part of the chicken fat and stock produced can be put aside for use in cooking other dishes. Chicken cooked in this way is invariably eaten only after it has been dipped in strong tasting sauces which are provided on the table. These dips are usually soya sauce based, with chopped ginger, garlic, spring onion, chilli, mustard, vinegar, sesame oil etc., blended into them. When dipped in these sauces the flavour of the plain-cooked chicken seems to be immediately lifted to a higher gastronomic level.

MENU A

Boiled chicken with Chinese cabbage
Mixed vegetable fried rice
Broccoli with oyster sauce

Boiled chicken with Chinese cabbage

Preparation: 6 minutes   Cooking: 1½ hours

---

1 small or medium-sized
  chicken
1 small or medium Chinese
  cabbage, about 1½ lb
  (750 g)
3 slices root ginger
½ tablespoon salt and pepper
1 chicken stock cube

For the dip
5 tablespoons dark soya sauce
2 teaspoons sesame oil
2 teaspoons chopped root
  ginger
3 teaspoons chopped spring
  onions

Preparation. Preheat oven to 200°C, 400°F, gas mark 6.
Plunge the chicken into boiling water, boil for 5 minutes,
then drain. Cut the cabbage through its bulk into 2–3
sections.

Cooking. Place the chicken in a deep casserole. Add 1¾
pints (1 litre) water, the ginger and salt and pepper. Cover
and cook in the oven for 50 minutes. Lift out the chicken.
Put the cabbage and crumbled stock cube in the casserole,
replace the chicken and cook in the oven for 20–25 minutes.

Serving. Bring the chicken to the table in the casserole. It
should be sufficiently tender to take to pieces with a pair of
chopsticks (if not, use a knife and fork). Mix the dip ingredients together, divide between 2 small dishes and place them
on 2 sides of the table for the convenience of the diners.

The diners would normally drink some of the soup and eat some of the cabbage before they tackle the chicken, which is dipped into the sauce, then eaten together with the rice.

Mixed vegetable fried rice

Preparation: 5 minutes   Cooking: 5 minutes

2 medium onions
2 tomatoes
2 young carrots
4 button mushrooms
2 spring onions
4 tablespoons vegetable oil
3–4 tablespoons green peas
  (fresh or frozen)

salt and pepper to taste
3 tablespoons chicken stock
  and fat
1 lb (450 g) cooked rice
1½ tablespoons soya sauce

Preparation. Cut the onion and tomatoes into thin slices and then into quarters. Chop the carrots and mushrooms into ½ inch (1 cm) cubes and the spring onions into shavings.

Cooking. Heat the oil in a wok, frying pan or casserole (preferably a casserole). Add the onions and carrots, stir-fry for 1½ minutes, then leave to cook for 1½ minutes. Add the mushrooms, peas and tomato, salt and pepper, chicken stock and fat. Bring to the boil and stir for 1 minute. Add the cooked rice, then stir together for 1½ minutes. Leave to stand over a low heat for ½ minute.

Serving. Sprinkle the top of the fried rice with spring onion shavings and soya sauce and, if cooked in a casserole, bring it to the table, otherwise transfer to a serving dish.

Broccoli with oyster sauce

Preparation: 3 minutes   Cooking: 6 minutes

¾ lb (350 g) broccoli
2 tablespoons vegetable oil
1 teaspoon salt

4 tablespoons chicken stock
   and fat
2 tablespoons oyster sauce

Preparation. Break the broccoli into florets and cut the roots and leaves into 1 inch (2 cm) pieces.

Cooking. Heat the oil in a saucepan. Add the broccoli and salt and stir together in the pan for 1 minute. Add the oyster sauce and chicken stock and fat. Stir, then leave to cook over a low to medium heat for 4–5 minutes.

Serving. Serve in a well-heated dish for the diners to help themselves from at the dining table.

MENU B

FOR 4–6 PEOPLE

Chicken braised in soya sauce
White-cooked leeks
Brown rice with mushrooms

Chicken braised in soya sauce

Preparation: 3–4 minutes   Cooking: 1 hour

---

1 medium-sized chicken
3–4 slices root ginger
4–5 tablespoons soya sauce
1 tablespoon sugar

4–5 tablespoons white or red
  wine, or sherry
salt and pepper to taste

Preparation. Heat the oven to 200°C, 400°F, gas mark 6. Chop the chicken through the bones into 10 or 12 pieces. Plunge them into a pan containing 2 pints (1.2 litres) of boiling water and boil for 10 minutes.

Cooking. Transfer the chicken and ½ pint (300 ml) of the cooking water to a casserole. Retain ½ pint (300 ml) of the remaining liquid for cooking the vegetables. Add the ginger, soya sauce, sugar, wine and salt and pepper to the casserole. Bring to the boil, cover and cook in the oven for 30 minutes. Stir well and continue cooking at 190°C, 375°F, gas mark 5 for 15 minutes.

Serving. Serve by bringing the casserole to the table for the diners to help themselves.

White-cooked leeks

Preparation: 3 minutes   Cooking: 7 minutes

5–6 young leeks
1 chicken stock cube

**½ pint (300 ml) stock
reserved from parboiling
the chicken
salt and pepper to taste**

Preparation. Clean the leeks thoroughly under cold water.
Cut them lengthwise into 2 inch (5 cm) pieces. Dissolve the
crumbled stock cube in the chicken stock.

Cooking. Place the leeks in a frying pan or saucepan. Pour
in the chicken stock. Season with salt and plenty of pepper.
Bring to the boil, then cook over high heat until the liquid
in the pan has been reduced by just under half.

Serving. Transfer the vegetables and liquid in the pan to
a deep well-heated serving dish.

Brown rice with mushrooms

Cooking: 30 minutes

1 lb (450 g) brown rice
**½ lb (225 g) firm button
mushrooms**
1½ oz (40 g) butter

Preparation and cooking. Cook the rice in the usual way
by boiling it in twice its own volume of water for 20 minutes
when most of the water will have been absorbed. Clean the
mushrooms thoroughly and add to the hot rice, together
with the butter. Turn the heat off, cover tightly and allow
the contents to cook in their own heat for 10 minutes.

MENU C

FOR 4 PEOPLE

---

*Soya braised and deep-fried
five-spiced drumsticks
Brown rice with green peas and
buttered vegetables
Spinach and tou-fu soup*

Soya braised and deep-fried five-spiced drumsticks

Preparation: 3 minutes   Cooking: 30 minutes

8–10 chicken drumsticks
1½ teaspoon salt
pepper to taste
1½ teaspoons five-spice
  powder (or 3 pieces star
  anise)

½ pint (300 ml) vegetable oil
4–5 tablespoons soya sauce
2 tablespoons hoisin sauce
1½ tablespoons sugar
1 pint (600 ml) stock or water

Preparation. Cut a slit two-thirds of the way along either side of each of the drumsticks. Rub them with salt, pepper and five-spice powder.

Cooking. Heat 3 tablespoons of the vegetable oil in a wok or frying pan. Add the drumsticks and fry for 2 minutes, then add the remaining ingredients and bring to the boil, stirring continuously. Cook at a rolling boil for the next 20–22 minutes or until the liquid in the pan is reduced to 1/10th. The meat on the drumsticks should be tender enough to tear off or cut from the bone with ease, and the sauce will be very tasty. Just before serving, heat the remaining oil in a saucepan or frying pan. When the oil is very hot, quickly deep-fry the drumsticks for 3–4 minutes, which will make them very crispy all over. These chicken drumsticks are ideal to take on a picnic as they can be eaten hot or cold.

Brown rice with green peas and buttered vegetables

Preparation: 5 minutes   Cooking: 5 minutes

1 stick celery
½ medium red pepper
3 inch (7 cm) section
  cucumber or courgette
¼ avocado pear (optional)
2 medium tomatoes

3–4 tablespoons green peas
  (fresh or frozen)
2–3 oz (50–75 g) butter
1 lb (450 g) cooked brown rice
salt and pepper to taste
2–3 tablespoons dry sherry

Preparation and cooking. Chop the vegetables into double pea-sized cubes. Heat the butter in a large frying pan, add all the vegetables and stir for 2 minutes. Add the rice and toss with the hot vegetables until the rice is hot. Add salt and pepper to taste. Sprinkle with sherry.

Serving. Serve on a well-heated dish, or, if cooked in a casserole, in the casserole itself.

Spinach and tou-fu soup

Preparation: 5 minutes   Cooking: 6–7 minutes

Diners should find this soup a satisfying complement to the chicken drumsticks and the vegetable brown rice.

½ lb (225 g) young spinach
1–2 cakes bean curd
2 pints (1.2 litres) stock
1 chicken stock cube

salt and pepper to taste
1 tablespoon dry sherry
1 teaspoon sesame oil

Preparation. Cut or tear the spinach into small pieces, discarding any yellow leaves and tough stems. Wash under cold water. Cut the bean curd into 20–30 pieces.

Cooking. Heat the stock in a saucepan. Dissolve the stock cube in the stock. Bring to the boil, add the spinach, bean curd and salt and pepper. When contents have come back to the boil, reduce the heat and simmer for 4–5 minutes. Add sherry and sesame oil and serve.

MENU D

Soya-braised chicken drumsticks
Bean sprout noodles with shredded
mushrooms
Green jade soup

Soya-braised chicken drumsticks

Preparation: 5 minutes   Cooking: 25 minutes

8–10 chicken drumsticks
1½ teaspoons salt
pepper to taste
1 large or 2 medium onions
2–3 tablespoons vegetable oil
2 tablespoons soya sauce

1 tablespoon yellow bean
  sauce (optional)
1 pint (600 ml) good stock
1 tablespoon sugar
1 chicken stock cube

Preparation. Cut a 3 inch (7.5 cm) slit along 2 sides of the
bone of the drumstick to loosen the meat from the bone.
Plunge the drumsticks in a pan of boiling water for 4–5
minutes, then drain and rub them evenly with salt and
pepper. Cut the onion into thin slices.

Cooking. Heat the oil in a casserole. Add the drumsticks
and onions and stir-fry over high heat for 3–4 minutes. Add
the remaining ingredients and bring to the boil, stirring.
Continue to turn the contents slowly and cook over high
heat for 5–6 minutes. Cover and cook over high heat for 10
minutes. Remove the lid, turn the contents and continue
cooking for 5 more minutes or until the liquid has been
reduced and thickened to less than 1/10th of the original
volume.

Bean sprout noodles with shredded mushrooms

Preparation: 25 minutes   Cooking: 25 minutes

2 oz (50 g) Chinese dried
  mushrooms (optional)
¾–1 lb (350–450 g) Chinese
  noodles or spaghetti
¼ lb (100 g) firm button
  mushrooms
½ chicken stock cube

6 tablespoons chicken stock
1 medium onion
1–2 spring onions
3 tablespoons vegetable oil
½ lb (225 g) bean sprouts
2–3 tablespoons soya sauce

Preparation. Soak the dried mushrooms for 20 minutes, then drain. Boil the spaghetti for about 8–10 minutes, or the noodles for 6 minutes, then drain and rinse under running water. Cut the button mushrooms into matchstick strips. Dissolve the crumbled stock cube in the stock. Cut the onion into thin slices and the spring onions into shavings.

Cooking. Heat the oil in a saucepan. Add the onions and dried mushrooms and stir-fry over a high heat for 3–4 minutes. Add the bean sprouts and mushrooms and stir-fry for 2½ minutes. Add the noodles or spaghetti, soya sauce, chicken stock and stir together for 2–3 minutes or until well heated through. Sprinkle with spring onion shavings and serve.

Green jade soup

Preparation: 5 minutes   Cooking: 5 minutes

½ lb (225 g) fresh spinach
  leaves
1¾ pints (1 litre) stock
1 chicken stock cube
1½ tablespoons light soya
  sauce

1½ tablespoons cornflour
  (blended with 6 tablespoons
  water)
salt and pepper to taste
1 teaspoon sesame oil

Preparation. Finely chop the spinach or put it through a mincer.

Cooking. Heat the stock in a saucepan, add the crumbled stock cube and bring to the boil. Add the spinach, bring to the boil again, then add the soya sauce, blended cornflour and salt and pepper to taste. Sprinkle the top of the soup with sesame oil and serve, either in individual bowls or in a large soup tureen for the diners to help themselves. The soup should be served at the same time as the noodles and braised drumsticks.

MENU E

---

*Quick-fried sliced chicken with French
beans or Distilled chicken
Steamed rice with broccoli and
chopped ham
Hot and sour soup*

Quick-fried sliced chicken with French beans

Preparation: 8 minutes   Cooking: 5–6 minutes

½–¾ lb (225–350 g) chicken
  breast
salt and pepper to taste
1 tablespoon cornflour
1 egg white
¾ lb (350 g) French beans

3–4 tablespoons vegetable oil
1½ tablespoons light soya
  sauce
½ tablespoon chopped root
  ginger
2 tablespoons stock

Preparation. Cut the chicken meat with a sharp knife into small bite-sized pieces. Rub with salt, pepper and cornflour and dip in egg white. Top and tail the beans and cut each one in half. Parboil them for 5 minutes and drain.

Cooking. Heat the oil in a frying pan, add the chicken and cook, stirring for 2½ minutes. Remove the chicken and set aside. Add the beans to the pan, stir in the remainder of the oil, adding a little more if necessary, and cook for 1½ minutes. Sprinkle with soya sauce, chopped ginger and add the stock. Continue to stir-fry for 1½ minutes. Return the chicken to the pan and stir with the beans for another 1½ minutes, then serve.

Distilled chicken

Preparation: 30 minutes   Cooking: 1¼ hours

'Distilled Chicken', a dish of South-West China, is usually cooked in a special earthenware casserole with a spout extending into the pot from the base. Through this, steam enters the pot when placed over a pan of boiling water, and that is how the chicken is cooked – by steam trapped inside the closed pot, creating 'distilled water'. Since this pot is not easily obtainable, the same effect can be produced by simply arranging the chopped chicken and other ingredients in a deep heatproof basin, and standing it in 3–4 inches (7.5–10 cm) of boiling water in a large saucepan. An inverted bowl or plate, slightly smaller than the basin, should be placed on top of it, resting on two crossed or parallel chopsticks. When the water boils vigorously and the steam strikes the bowl or plate, there will be sufficient condensation dripping onto the chicken to cook it in 1–1¼ hours. The theme of this dish is one of purity.

1 chicken about 2–3 lbs (1 kg–1.25 kg)	2 spring onions
	2 dried chillis
5–6 medium Chinese dried mushrooms	2 teaspoons salt
	3 slices root ginger
3–4 oz (75–100 g) bamboo shoots	pepper to taste

Preparation. Chop the chicken through the bones into 20 pieces. Blanch in boiling water for 3–4 minutes and drain. Soak the dried mushrooms in hot water for 25 minutes. Remove the stems and cut the caps in half. Cut the bamboo shoots into 2 × 1 inch (5 × 2.5 cm) thin slices, and the spring onions into 2 inch (5 cm) pieces. Chop the chillis coarsely, discarding the seeds.

Cooking. Layer the chicken pieces, mushrooms, ginger, and bamboo shoots in a basin or special pot. Sprinkle with salt, pepper, spring onions and chillis. Stand the basin in a saucepan filled with 3–4 inches (7.5–10 cm) boiling water. Place a pair of chopsticks apart on top of the basin, and put an inverted bowl or plate on top of them. Bring the water to a vigorous boil and cook for 1–1¼ hours, replenishing with boiling water when necessary. Adjust the seasoning, judging partly by the amount of condensed water collected in the basin. A dash of white wine or sherry sprinkled over the dish would not go amiss.

Serving. Serve straight from the pot or basin. This is another one of China's 'semi-soup' dishes. The soup and vegetables are spooned on to the diners' rice in their respective rice bowls, and the chicken pieces picked up with chopsticks and dipped in good quality soya sauce before eating.

Steamed rice with broccoli and chopped ham

Preparation: 5 minutes   Cooking: 20 minutes

¾–1 lb (350–450 g) rice
½ lb (225 g) broccoli
¼ lb (100 g) cooked ham

Preparation. Wash the rice, then parboil it for 10 minutes and drain. Break the broccoli into 2 inch (5 cm) florets and cut the stalks into similar size pieces. Chop the ham coarsely.

Cooking. Put the rice in a large heatproof bowl or basin. Stud with the broccoli florets and bury the cut stalks in the rice. Put the bowl in a steamer and steam vigorously for 8–10 minutes.

Serving. Sprinkle the rice and broccoli with the chopped ham and serve on the table for the diners to help themselves.

Hot and sour soup

This is the one instance where the soup is more savoury than the meat dish. It is very warming in the winter and should be drunk during the meal along with the rice and chicken and vegetable dish.

2 tablespoons dried shrimps
5–6 tablespoons dried mushrooms
10 tablespoons boiling water
1–2 rashers bacon
1 medium onion
1 egg
2 tablespoons vegetable oil
1¾ pints (1 litre) stock
2 chicken stock cubes
5–6 tablespoons button mushrooms

2 tablespoons soya sauce
6 tablespoons shelled shrimps
1 teaspoon salt
½ teaspoon black pepper
3 tablespoons wine vinegar
2 tablespoons cornflour (blended with 6 tablespoons water)
½ tablespoon sesame oil

Preparation. Soak the dried shrimps and dried mushrooms in the boiling water for 15 minutes. Drain and keep the water. Cut the bacon into shreds, having removed the rind. Thinly slice the onion. Beat the egg lightly.

Cooking. Heat the oil in a saucepan. Add the dried shrimps and dried mushrooms, onion and bacon and stir-fry in the hot oil for 1½ minutes. Pour in the stock and add the crumbled stock cubes, mushrooms, mushroom water, soya sauce, shrimps, salt and pepper. Bring to the boil, then simmer gently for 10 minutes. Stir in the vinegar and blended cornflour to thicken the soup. Adjust the seasonings. Add the beaten egg by pouring it very slowly along the prongs of a fork to trail over the surface of the soup. When the egg has set, give the soup a stir and sprinkle the surface with sesame oil and serve.

MENU F

FOR 4 PEOPLE

*Shangtung hand-shredded spiced
chicken*
Stir-fried egg with tomato
Shredded cucumber soup with shrimps

Shangtung hand-shredded spiced chicken

Preparation: 8 minutes   Cooking: 25 minutes

half a medium chicken
salt and pepper to taste

For the sauce
1 tablespoon finely chopped
  root ginger
2 tablespoons coarsely
  chopped spring onions

2 tablespoons soya sauce
2 tablespoons vinegar
3 tablespoons good stock
1 tablespoon vegetable oil
¼ tablespoon sesame oil

Preparation. Preheat oven to 200°C, 400°F, gas mark 6.
Rub the chicken with plenty of salt and pepper. Chop the
ginger and spring onions as indicated.

Cooking. Put the half chicken on a wire rack in a tin half-
filled with water and roast in the oven for 25 minutes. Turn
off the heat and leave the chicken to cool.

Serving. When the chicken has cooled sufficiently to
handle easily, detach all the meat from the bones and shred
by hand into triple matchstick shreds. Pile the shredded
chicken on a serving dish. Blend the sauce ingredients in a
bowl and pour the sauce over the chicken before serving.

97

Stir-fried egg with tomato

Preparation: 5 minutes   Cooking: 5 minutes

The addition of sherry towards the final stages of cooking endows this dish with a fragrant bouquet.

4 eggs
salt and pepper to taste
3 medium tomatoes
1 medium onion

4 tablespoons vegetable oil
2 tablespoons dry sherry
2 tablespoons soya sauce

Preparation. Beat the eggs lightly in a bowl with salt and pepper. Cut the tomatoes into thin slices and each slice into quarters. Cut the onion into very thin slices.

Cooking. Heat the oil in a frying pan. Add the onions and stir-fry them for 1½ minutes. Add the tomato pieces and spread them out evenly. Pour in the beaten eggs, between the pieces of tomato. When the eggs have set pour the sherry evenly over the egg and tomato. Stir and scramble the egg and tomatoes together lightly, breaking them into large chunky pieces. Transfer the mixture to a serving dish, sprinkle with soya sauce and serve.

Shredded cucumber soup with shrimps

Preparation: 15 minutes   Cooking: 20 minutes

1½ tablespoons dried shrimps
1 medium cucumber (about 12
   inch (30 cm))
1¾ pints (1 litre) good stock
1 chicken stock cube

1 tablespoon root ginger,
   finely chopped
salt and pepper to taste
2–3 tablespoons fresh or
   cooked shrimps

Preparation. Soak the dried shrimps in a small bowl of boiling water for 15 minutes. Quarter the cucumber, then slice into triple matchstick pieces.

Cooking. Bring the stock to the boil in a saucepan. Add

the soaked dried shrimps and shrimp water, crumbled stock cube and chopped ginger. Reduce the heat and simmer gently for 10 minutes. Season with salt and pepper. Add the fresh or cooked shrimps and shredded cucumber. Simmer for 3–4 minutes, then serve.

DUCK

After chicken, duck is the most popular and widely eaten poultry in China. The flavour of its meat is gamier than that of chicken, therefore it is usually eaten dipped in a sauce with a pronounced taste such as 'Peking Duck Sauce' or a mustard sauce. The most popular duck dish along the Yangtze River is 'Nanking Salt-Water Duck'. It is said that some 40 million ducks are produced in and around Nanking annually. But the most famous Chinese duck dish is undoubtedly the 'Peking Duck' which is much easier to make than one would have believed. It is a case of straightforward roasting, which makes it much easier to cook in the average Western kitchen than in a typical Chinese kitchen since hardly any Chinese kitchen is equipped with an oven, while they are standard equipment in any Western kitchen. Another favourite is the 'Szechuan Aromatic and Crispy Duck'. The duck is seasoned with ginger, salt, pepper and spring onion and 'five spices' for several hours or overnight, then steamed for a couple of hours to tenderize the flesh and reduce the fat (allowing the latter to drain away or put aside for other uses). It is then cooled and, when needed for a meal, deep-fried in hot oil for about 10 minutes. This achieves its final crispness. The recipe is not given here, as the oil required for the cooking is excessive and therefore not conducive to good health. Instead we shall start with 'Peking Duck', which is quite simple.

MENU A

FOR 4–5 PEOPLE

Peking duck
Duck carcass and cabbage soup
Brown rice with mushrooms (page 86)

Peking Duck

Preparation: 20 minutes, plus drying overnight
Cooking: 1¼ hours

---

1 medium duck (3½–4 lbs
   (1.5–1.75 kg))
½ medium cucumber
4 spring onions

5 tablespoons sugar
5 tablespoons vegetable oil
6 tablespoons water
½ tablespoon sesame oil

For the sauce
5 tablespoons yellow bean
   sauce

Preparation. Preheat oven to 200°C, 400°F, gas mark 6.
Clean the duck with damp kitchen paper, then hang it up to
dry in an airy place overnight. Cut the cucumber into matchstick strips (leaving the skin on). Cut the spring onions into
thin shreds co about the same length as the cucumber strips.
Prepare the sauce by blending all the sauce ingredients
together, except the sesame oil.

Put the sauce ingredients in a small heavy saucepan, bring
to the boil, then, reduce the heat and stir for 3–4 minutes,
when most of the water will have evaporated. Add the sesame
oil and stir for another 15 seconds. Leave to cool.

Cooking. Place the duck on a wire rack in a roasting tin
quarter filled with water. Roast in the oven for 15 minutes,

then reduce the heat to 190°C, 375°F, gas mark 5 and continue roasting for 1 hour when the duck will be ready to serve.

Serving. Divide the sauce, shredded cucumber and spring onion into 2 dishes. Remove the skin from the duck with a sharp knife and arrange the pieces on a well-heated dish. Carve the duck meat and arrange on another serving dish. Put the pancakes on a third dish.

Eating. To eat Peking Duck, dip the skin and meat in the sauce so they are well covered. Put the pieces on a pancake, top with a large pinch each of shredded cucumber and spring onion, then roll up the pancakes so that they can be picked up with the fingers. The pleasure of eating the dish lies in the enjoyment of biting through the crispness of the skin, the meatiness of the meat and the crunchiness of the fresh vegetables, amply laced with the piquant sauce. If the pancakes are not available, they can be substituted with thinly sliced brown bread.

Pancakes

Preparation: 30 minutes   Cooking: 40 minutes

1 lb (450 g) plain flour	8 fl oz (250 ml) warm water
2 teaspoons sugar	sesame oil
1½ teaspoons oil	

Preparation. Sift the flour into a mixing bowl. Stir in the sugar, oil and warm water. Stir with a wooden spoon until well mixed. Knead the mixture into a firm dough, then form into 2 large sausage-shaped strips. Cut each strip into 12 pieces, and shape each piece into a small ball. Flatten each ball with the palm into a round disc. Brush the top of one of the discs with sesame oil, and place a second disc on top to form a sandwich. Roll out the dough into a pancake of about 5–6 inches (13–15 cm) diameter. Repeat until you have used up all the dough.

Cooking. Heat a dry frying pan over low heat. Place a pancake in the pan, and shake it so that the pancake slides around on the surface of the pan. After 2 minutes turn the pancake over with a fish-slice and cook the other side in the same manner for 1½ minutes until the pancake begins to puff and bubble slightly. The pancake is ready when some brown spots begin to appear on the underside. Carefully peel off the top pancake. Fold each pancake in half, and stack them up. If they are not used immediately cover them with a damp cloth. They can be reheated by placing them in a steamer for a couple of minutes.

Duck carcass and cabbage soup

This soup is just what it says, and is simply prepared. Chop the carcass into 4 pieces and boil them in 2–3 pints (1.2–1.75 litres) water with a small Chinese cabbage (cut into 12 pieces) and 1 or 2 crumbled chicken stock cubes. When the contents come to the boil, reduce the heat, adjust the seasoning and simmer gently for 18–20 minutes. Since the 'Peking Duck' is a rich dish, the soup to complement it should not be made over-savoury.

Brown rice with mushrooms

This dish is required only if the previous 2 dishes are found to be not sufficiently filling for 4–5 people.

MENU B

FOR 4–5 PEOPLE

Nanking salt-water duck
Brown rice with green peas and
buttered chopped vegetables (page 88)
Green jade soup (page 91)

Nanking salt-water duck

Preparation: 1 hour   Cooking: 30 minutes
Seasoning: overnight

---

1 medium duck (3½–4 lb
  (1.5–1.75 kg))
¾ tablespoon salt
1½ tablespoons finely
  chopped root ginger

For the boiling stock
3 pints (1.75 litres) stock
6 slices root ginger
3 cloves garlic, crushed
1¼ tablespoons salt
2 chicken stock cubes
1 tablespoon star anise

1 lb (450 g) spare ribs
2 medium onions

For the dipping sauce
2 spring onions, finely
  chopped
1½ tablespoons mustard
  powder (blended with 3
  tablespoons water)
3 tablspoons stock
2 tablespoons wine vinegar
2 tablespoons light soya sauce
1 tablespoon vegetable oil

Preparation. Plunge the duck into a large pan of boiling
water. Boil for 10 minutes, then drain. When cool, rub the
duck inside and out with salt and ginger, then leave for at
least 4 hours or overnight. Place all the ingredients for the
boiling stock in a saucepan. Bring to the boil, then simmer
gently for 40 minutes. Strain and reserve the stock and spare-

ribs (which may be eaten with the duck, using some of the dip). Mix together the ingredients for the dipping sauce.

Cooking. Bring the stock to the boil, add the duck, bring back to the boil and cook 7–8 minutes. Turn off the heat. When the stock has cooled to a point where one can stick a finger in it, bring to the boil again and cook for another 7 minutes. Allow to cool in the same way. Repeat the process once more, then leave the duck to cool completely in the liquid.

Serving. Remove the duck from the stock and chop through the bones into large bite-sized pieces. Divide the 'dipping sauce' between 2 saucer-sized dishes. Dip the pieces of duck into the sauce before eating. As the duck meat has not been overcooked, it should be firm and juicy. This duck is normally served cold; it is therefore essential to serve a hot soup with it. The brown rice with vegetables is meant to act as a supplement and a filler, since meat on its own to us Chinese does not constitute a complete Chinese meal.

MENU C

FOR 4–5 PEOPLE

Tangerine duck
Mixed vegetable fried rice (page 83)
Broccoli with oyster sauce (page 84)

Tangerine duck

Preparation: 30 minutes   Cooking: 1 hour

3¼ lb (1.5 kg) duck
4 tablespoons dried tangerine
  peel
4 slices root ginger
3 tablespoons light soya sauce
2 tablespoons dark soya sauce

½ pint (300 ml) good stock
¼ pint (150 ml) red wine
1 tablespoon sugar
¼ teaspoon Sichuan pepper
  (or 1/3 teaspoon black
  pepper)

Preparation. Preheat oven to 200°C, 400°F, gas mark 6. If using fresh duck, clean the duck and remove oil sac from the tail end. Dismember the duck and chop it through the bone into 20–24 bite-sized pieces. Plunge the pieces into a pan of boiling water to blanch for 6 minutes and drain. Soak the tangerine peel in warm water for 20 minutes and drain.

Cooking. Place the duck pieces in a casserole. Add the remaining ingredients and bring to the boil. Stir thoroughly, then cover and cook in the oven for 20 minutes. Reduce the heat to 180°C, 350°F, gas mark 4, and cook for a further 40 minutes.

Serving. Serve straight from the casserole.

RICE

Rice in a Chinese meal serves mainly as a bulk food, which stands between the savoury meat dish and the fresh vegetable dish. It is generally served plain and cooked in an uncomplicated way. As a dish within a meal, it does not vie with the flavour of the meat and vegetables, as it is there mainly to lend weight to a meal. However, there are instances when rice dishes have to stand on their own as a complete meal. In these cases they have to combine something of both the meat and vegetable dishes. If an accompaniment is required for such an independent rice dish, in China it is often a tou-fu (bean curd) dish. The appreciation of tou-fu is largely a cultivated taste, because it is rather bland, but once one learns to appreciate it, one is likely to enjoy it unswervingly for the rest of one's life (most Japanese are great appreciators of tou-fu). It also adds a certain amount of nutritional value to a meal.

MENU A

FOR 3–4 PEOPLE

Basic vegetarian fried rice
Cold-tossed bean curd

Basic vegetarian fried rice

Preparation: 5 minutes   Cooking: 6–7 minutes

2 medium onions
2 oz (50 g) Chinese 'snow
  pickles' (or salted turnips
  or gherkins)
3 eggs
4 tablespoons vegetable oil
1 lb (450 g) cooked rice

For later addition
3 inch (7.5 cm) piece cucumber
½ medium red pepper
3–4 leaves crisp lettuce
  (Iceberg)
2 medium tomatoes
2 tablespoons vegetable oil
4 tablespoons green peas
  (fresh or frozen)
2 tablespoons light soya sauce
1 teaspoon sesame oil

Preparation. Thinly slice the onions and cut the pickles into small cubes (pea size). Beat the eggs lightly in a bowl. Dice the cucumber and red pepper into ½ inch (1 cm) cubes; cut the lettuce into 1–1½ inch (2.5–4 cm) pieces and each tomato into 6 pieces.

Cooking. Heat the oil in a large frying pan. Add the onion and stir over medium heat for 2 minutes. Pour in the beaten egg. Tilt the pan so the egg flows evenly over the surface of the pan. When the egg is about to set, sprinkle on the pickles. Once the eggs have set, scramble the contents lightly. Add the rice, and mix with all the ingredients in the pan. Heat the rest of the oil in a saucepan. Add the peas, tomatoes, peppers, cucumber and lettuce. Stir a few times and sprinkle with soya sauce and sesame oil. Turn the contents over a couple more times and empty them all over the rice mixture in the frying pan. Mix all the ingredients together lightly.

Serving. The dish should be served hot in a well-heated serving dish or even in a casserole, especially when it is meant to be accompanied by a cold dish.

Cold-tossed bean curd

Preparation: 10 minutes

The excellent flavour of this dish, and the fact that it is made from very inexpensive ingredients, makes it certainly one of the most widely served dishes throughout China. It is usually served at breakfast time or for a midnight supper, and is thoroughly enjoyed by people of all classes and persuasions in China.

3 cakes bean curd

For the sauce
1 tablespoon finely chopped root ginger
1 tablespoon finely chopped Hot Szechuan Ja Chai pickles (or gherkins)
1 tablespoon finely chopped garlic
1 tablespoon finely chopped Chinese 'snow pickles' (or chutney)

1½ tablespoons chopped dried shrimps (previously soaked in water 1 hour)
1½ tablespoons chopped spring onions
2½ tablespoons dark soya sauce
2½ tablespoons wine vinegar
1 tablespoon sesame oil

Preparation and serving. Cut each bean curd cake into 12 pieces and place in a deep dish. Mix all the sauce ingredients together and sprinkle evenly over the bean curd. A mouthful of Vegetarian Fried Rice goes down very enjoyably with bean curd and this mixed ingredient sauce. The conjunction of hot rice with cold bean curd conveys an unusual yet satisfying gastronomic sensation to the palate.

MENU B

Basic egg and bacon fried rice
Szechuan ma-po hot-tossed bean curd

Basic egg and bacon fried rice

Preparation: 5–6 minutes   Cooking: 5–6 minutes

Egg and Bacon Fried Rice is prepared in basically the same way as the Vegetarian Fried Rice (page 110), except perhaps more simply. Once bacon is introduced as an ingredient, we have all the saltiness needed for the dish and can, therefore, dispense with the pickles. The fresh vegetables used in the cooking can also be reduced from 4–3 without detracting much from the quality and character of the dish.

4 rashers bacon	*For later addition*
2 medium onions	4 medium tomatoes
3–4 eggs	3–4 crisp lettuce leaves
4 tablespoons vegetable oil	2 tablespoons vegetable oil
4 tablespoons green peas	2 tablespoons light soya sauce
(fresh or frozen)	1 tablespoon wine vinegar
1 lb (450 g) cooked rice	½ tablespoon sesame oil

Preparation. Cut the bacon into matchstick shreds, after removing the rind. Thinly slice the onions, and cut each tomato into 6 slices. Cut the lettuce into 1–1½ inch (2.5–4 cm) size pieces. Beat the eggs lightly in a bowl.

Cooking. Heat the oil in a large frying pan. Add the onions and bacon and stir-fry for 2 minutes. Pour the egg evenly into the pan and sprinkle with green peas. When the eggs have set, add the cooked rice, and turn and mix evenly with all the other ingredients. Heat the oil in a saucepan, add the tomatoes and lettuce and sprinkle with soya sauce and vinegar. Stir a few times. Empty the contents of the saucepan over the rice in the frying pan. Heat through, stirring, until the rice is hot. Sprinkle with sesame oil.

Serving. Serve on a well-heated dish to be eaten with the following bean curd dish.

Szechuan ma-po hot-tossed bean curd

Preparation: 35 minutes   Cooking: 15 minutes

This is a famous Szechuan dish. In Chinese it is simply called 'The Pock-Marked Housewife's Bean Curd'! It is mainly a combination of minced meat and bean curd, and because a good amount of chilli and black beans are added during the cooking, it is a hot dish with a strong character.

3 tablespoons Chinese dried shrimps
4 medium dried mushrooms
1½ tablespoons salted black beans
2 dried chillis
2 fresh chillis
3 cakes bean curd
1 medium onion

2 cloves garlic
5 tablespoons vegetable oil
1 teaspoon salt
1 lb (450 g) minced meat (pork or beef)
soya sauce
2 tablespoons cornflour (blended with 8 tablespoons good stock)

Preparation. Soak the dried shrimps and mushrooms in water for 30 minutes. Drain and chop coarsely, having removed the stems from mushrooms. Soak the black beans in water for 3–4 minutes. Drain and chop coarsely. Finely chop the chillis, having discarded the seeds. Cut each bean curd into 12 pieces. Cut the onion and garlic into thin slices.

Cooking. Heat the oil in a frying pan. Add the onion, garlic and salt and stir-fry over high heat for 1½ minutes. Add the chillis, dried shrimps and mushrooms and stir-fry for 2 minutes. Add the minced meat and black beans and continue to cook, stirring, until the meat has cooked through

113

and turned brown (about 4 minutes). Stir in the soya sauce. Bring to the boil, reduce the heat and simmer for 5 minutes. Pour in the blended cornflour and increase the heat to high. Stir until the contents thicken.

Serving. Serve in a deep dish for the diners to help themselves with spoonfuls of this hot spicy dish to eat with quantities of rice or fried rice. Because of the spiciness of this dish which works on the taste-buds, few people know when to stop once they tuck into it!

CONGEE

Congee, or soft rice, is usually eaten in China for breakfast, accompanied by salted, pickled or nutty foods. When it is eaten for breakfast, it is always cooked plain and watery. In this state it imparts a refreshing feel to the mouth, and the heat in the rice (like hot tea) helps you to wake up!

When soft rice is flavoured (by cooking meat, seafood or fish in it), it is always served as a self-contained snack, often eaten at teatime or as a light supper. Because of the way the rice is cooked (gently boiled with ample water), such snacks are easily digested. Thus, soft rice is often served to invalids or the elderly whose digestive powers are not at their peak.

MENU A

---

*Gold and silver congee with chicken
and duck
Chinese smoked fish*

Gold and silver congee with chicken and duck

Preparation: 10 minutes   Cooking: 2 hours

½ lb (225 g) rice
4–5 oz (100–150 g) chicken
  meat (boiled)
4–5 oz (100–150 g) duck meat
  (roasted or soya-braised)

4–5 oz (100–150 g) young leeks
1 small cauliflower
1 chicken stock cube

Preparation. Cut the duck and chicken meat into 10 thin slices each. Wash the leeks thoroughly and cut slantwise into 1 inch (2.5 cm) sections. Break the cauliflower roughly into 2–3 inch (5–7.5 cm) florets.

Cooking. Wash the rice, then place in a large saucepan with 3 pints (1.75 litres) of water. Bring to the boil, reduce the heat to very low and simmer gently for 1½ hours, stirring every 15 minutes. Add the chicken, duck and vegetables to the rice, distributing them evenly. Crumble in the stock cube. Bring to the boil, reduce the heat to very low and simmer gently for 15 minutes, stirring every 5 minutes.

Serving. Ladle the mixture into individual rice bowls. The soft rice is meant to be mildly flavoured, to keep it refreshing. The diner is recommended to add ¾ tablespoon of soya sauce into his bowl before commencing to eat. He is not recommended to stir and mix it evenly into the rice; the interest lies in having some mouthfuls of plain soft rice and some flavoured by soya sauce.

Chinese smoked fish

Preparation: 8 minutes   Cooking: 6 minutes

1lb (450 g) fish fillets (cod, halibut, plaice, sole or bream)
1½ teaspoons salt
pepper to taste
1 egg white
4 tablespoons cornflour
oil to deep-fry

For the sauce
1 tablespoon chopped root ginger
1½ tablespoons sugar
1 tablespoon chilli sauce
1 tablespoon finely chopped spring onion
1 tablespoon wine vinegar
2 tablespoons dry sherry
4 tablespoons dark soya sauce

Preparation. Rub the fish with salt and pepper. Blend the beaten egg with the cornflour into a batter. Coat the fish evenly with the batter. Mix all the sauce ingredients together in a large dish, stirring until well blended.

Cooking. Heat 1 inch (2.5 cm) oil in a frying pan. Lay the fish carefully in the pan and fry over medium heat for 3 minutes on each side. Remove and drain, and place, while still hot, in the dish of sauce. Turn the fish over a few times so that it is evenly sauced. Leave for at least 15 minutes, until cold.

Serving. Remove the fish from the sauce and cut into 12 regular pieces. Two or three pieces are sufficient to accompany a bowl of savoury soft rice.

MENU B

FOR 4 PEOPLE

Fish and seafood congee
Cold-cut soya meat

Fish and seafood congee

Preparation: 1¼ hours   Cooking: 20 minutes

½ lb (225 g) rice
½ lb (225 g) fish fillets (cod,
  bream, halibut or turbot)
1½ teaspoons salt
8 small oysters or poached
  mussels
1 tablespoon wine vinegar

2 sticks celery
3 spring onions
4–5 oz (100–150 g) peeled
  prawns (fresh or frozen)
3–4 slices root ginger
1 chicken stock cube

Preparation. Boil the rice in the same way as for Gold
and Silver Congee (page 115). Rub the fish with salt and leave
for 30 minutes, then cut into regular sized pieces. Remove the
shellfish from the shells and sprinkle with vinegar. Clean and
cut the celery and spring onions into 1 inch (2.5 cm) lengths.

Cooking. Add the fish, mussels or oysters, prawns, ginger,
spring onions, celery and crumbled stock cube to the soft
rice. Bring to the boil and immediately reduce the heat to
low. Stir well, then simmer gently for 15 minutes.

Serving. Serve in individual bowls, sprinkling 2 teaspoons
soya sauce over each bowl. The following dish of Cold-Cut
Soya Meat is excellent to serve with it.

117

Cold-cut soya meat

1 lb (450 g) meat (pork, lamb or beef)	2–3 oz (50–75 g) pork skin
2 spring onions	1 tablespoon sugar
2 cloves garlic	1 tablespoon chilli sauce
3 slices root ginger	1 tablespoon hoisin sauce (optional)
1 medium onion	1 glass red wine
1½ pints (900 ml) stock or water	4 tablespoons dark soya sauce

Preparation and cooking. Cut the meat into 1½–2 inch (4–5 cm) thick strips. Coarsely chop the spring onions and thinly slice the garlic, ginger and onion. Bring the stock or water to the boil in a saucepan or casserole. Add the meat, pork skin, ginger, garlic and onion. When the contents boil again, reduce the heat to low and simmer for 40 minutes. Lift out the meat and remove all the other solids with a perforated spoon. Return the meat to the pan. Add the sugar, chilli sauce, hoisin sauce, soya sauce and wine. Bring to the boil again, reduce the heat to low and simmer gently for 30 minutes. Leave the meat to cool in the pan. When cool, pour into a deep dish and chill in the refrigerator for 1½ hours, when the sauce will have set into a jelly.

Serving. Lift the meat from the jelly, place on a chopping board and cut into ¼ inch (5 mm) thick slices across the grain. Arrange in the centre of a serving dish. Remove the fat from the top of the jelly and spoon the jelly around the sliced meat. Sprinkle with chopped spring onion and serve.

To eat with soft rice, spoon a piece of cold-cut meat together with an equal amount of meat jelly on top of the rice. From the health point of view, it is the experience of us Chinese that almost any main dish (braised, roasted, fried, stir-fried) tends to become more digestible when eaten with a copious amount of congee or soft rice. When meat and fish are not available, the other items suitable for accompanying soft rice are: soya eggs, salt-eggs, pickles and/or Chinese salami wind-dried sausages.

MENU C

Steamed sampan soft rice with soya egg and chopped spring cabbage

---

Preparation: 7–8 minutes   Cooking: 15 minutes
Marinating: 1 hour

This is a self-contained dish – which needs no supplementary dish to go with it. It should be served in 4 extra-large bowls or basins which are used both in the cooking and the serving.

¾ lb (350 g) fish fillets
6 tablespoons peeled shrimps (fresh or frozen)
6 tablespoons clam meat (fresh, frozen or boiled) (optional)
1 lb (450 g) spring cabbage
4 large bowls (3½ litres) soft rice
4 tablespoons chopped spring onion

1 teaspoon salt
4 soya eggs (page 134)

Marinade for fish and seafoods
3 tablespoons soya sauce
2 tablespoons chopped root ginger
1 tablespoon wine vinegar
1 tablespoon vegetable oil
½ tablespoon sesame oil

Preparation. Cut the fish into 16 pieces and place in a dish with the shrimps and clam meat (if using). Add all the marinade ingredients, mix well and leave for 1 hour. Remove and discard the tough or discoloured outer leaves of the spring cabbage and chop the heart into bite-sized pieces. Heat the pre-cooked soft rice until about to boil.

Cooking. Divide the cabbage and spring onions equally between the 4 bowls. Sprinkle with salt, and pour over the fish marinade. Divide the hot soft rice equally between the bowls. Place a soya egg on one side of the soft rice in each of the four bowls, then place the fish and seafoods on the other side and in the centre. Place the bowls in a steamer and steam for 12 minutes.

Serving. Remove the bowls from the steamer and serve immediately. Since the bowls are very hot, the diners are advised to commence eating only after a few minutes have elapsed. Such bowls of soft rice are not only self-contained but well-balanced nutritionally, apart from being enjoyable to eat. The contrast of flavour and texture of the soft rice with the other ingredients in the bowl make this altogether a most nourishing dish.

MENU D

The beggars' soft rice

Preparation: 6 minutes   Cooking: 12 minutes

The poorer strata of the Chinese population in the past seldom ate rice cooked firm and dry, as it is normally served in Chinese restaurants abroad. They usually ate 'soft rice' into which a larger than usual amount of water had been added – in fact it was 'watery soft rice'. If one went further down the poverty line, one ate 'watery soft rice' into which shredded sweet potato had been added or chopped vegetable roots and leaves. Yet nutritionally, 'soft rice' so prepared and cooked does not deserve to be dismissed out of hand.

1 large sweet potato
¾–1 lb (350–450 g)
  cauliflower leaves and stems
2 teaspoons salt
2 tablespoons vegetable oil
4 large bowls (3½ pints)
  (2 litres) soft rice

5 tablespoons peanut butter
5 tablespoons soya sauce
4–5 tablespoons finely
  chopped spring onions

Preparation. Peel and cut the sweet potato into triple matchstick pieces. Clean, trim and cut the cauliflower leaves and stems into bite-sized pieces (discarding any discoloured and overtough parts). Divide the sweet potato and cauliflower between 4 large serving bowls or basins. Sprinkle with salt and oil. Place the soft rice on top of the vegetables, filling the bowls to the brim.

Cooking. Place the bowls in a steamer and steam for 10–12 minutes.

Serving. Remove the bowls from the steamer and place

them in front of each diner. Put a large dollop of peanut butter on top of each bowl of soft rice, then sprinkle over the soya sauce and chopped spring onion. The peanut butter and spring onion are together nutty and aromatic when added to the salty-savouriness of soya sauce, and when they are stirred into the soft rice and vegetables, they make the bowls of food both satisfying and enjoyable to consume. Since cauliflower stems and leaves can usually be obtained for nothing, and peanut butter and soya sauce of the quantity required are by no means expensive, such bowls of soft rice can be very economical.

MENU E

Beggars' boiled noodles

Preparation and cooking: 15 minutes

A similar self-contained dish as the previous recipe can be cooked with noodles instead of rice. It is more popular and just as widely eaten as the rice version, being a favourite snack among the bourgeoisie of China. Incredibly, it has recently become popular in the United States and there are several Chinese restaurants in New York which have become well known for serving just this version of noodles. Indeed, during my gastronomic tour of China earlier this year, we encountered this dish in the upland city of Kunming in South West China, and this version of 'Beggars' Noodles' was very much appreciated by some well-heeled fellow-travellers from Monte Carlo!

6 inch (15 cm) section of cucumber

1½ lb (750 g) Chinese noodles or spaghetti

4 tablespoons finely chopped spring onion

5 tablespoons peanut butter

5 tablespoons soya sauce

5 tablespoons good stock

2½ tablespoons chilli sauce

Preparation and cooking. Cut the cucumber into double matchstick shreds. Boil the noodles for 5 minutes or spaghetti for 8–10 minutes and drain. While still hot, divide between 4 large bowls. Sprinkle with chopped spring onions and place a large dollop of peanut butter on top. Pour over the soya sauce, then the stock. Place the shredded cucumber on one side of the peanut butter, and a small dollop of chilli sauce on the other.

Serving. The diner commences by mixing the ingredients, a little at a time (instead of mixing all the ingredients together at once), proceeding from mouthful to mouthful. Because of the hot spiciness and nuttiness of the ingredients, and the sumptuousness of the noodles, one often feels one can go on eating for ever!

NOODLES

Noodles are eaten extensively in China. They are usually plainly cooked and eaten in conjunction with two or three other savoury dishes, except in the South where they are more often eaten as a snack. In the North where much more wheat, millet and maize are grown and ground into flours which is then made into noodles, they are often cooked and served as a bulk food for main meals instead of rice. Unlike rice, however, noodles are seldom served plain. After cooking, interesting ingredients are added or tossed into them to make them complete dishes, which can be eaten as a meal on their own. Only on more festive occasions will noodles be supported by one or two other dishes to make a more extensive meal.

The basic way in which noodles are made more appetizing in Chinese cooking is to cook a small amount of ingredients, such as dried shrimps, mushrooms, pickled vegetables, salted meats, and onion in a small amount of oil. After a short period of stir-frying together, when the flavours of these strong-tasting ingredients have been imparted into the oil, this 'flavoured oil' is then in turn used to toss with the parboiled noodles. To make the flavour even more interesting, shredded meats, fresh vegetables and seafoods are often stir-fried separately, along with good stock, wine and soya sauce. These are then added to the noodles as garnish, allowing the gravy, a freshly composed 'sauce', to seep down through the noodles to provide a more sophisticated flavour (a compound of the rich with the fresh).

In cases where quantities of stock and liquid ingredients are added in the second stage of the cooking, the noodles may then be cooked for a longer period in a pot with the sauce. Such noodles are called 'sauce noodles' (tu mein) or 'pot-cooked noodles' (wo mein). They are most often served in the winter as a warming dish. When noodles are added or cooked in soups – usually clear consommés with light, fresh, shredded ingredients – they become 'soup noodles' with which the West is better acquainted, as they are often served as soup and as a part of a course, of a multi-course meal.

There are only a few instances where a thick meat sauce is combined with plain-cooked noodles. They are tossed and stirred together (in the Italian fashion such as 'Spaghetti Bolognese'). The following dish is a very popular one in Peking and is an instance of this type of noodles. In addition to the meat sauce, some cut shredded raw vegetables are also tossed onto the noodles, which makes the dish more appealing from the health point of view as well as looking very attractive.

MENU A

FOR 3–4 PEOPLE

Peking ja jiang mein noodles
Egg flower soup with tomatoes

Peking ja jiang mein noodles

Preparation: 15 minutes Cooking: 20 minutes

1 lb (450 g) Chinese noodles or
  spaghetti
½ lb (225 g) bean sprouts
3–4 spring onions
3 medium young carrots

For the meat sauce
4 tablespoons vegetable oil
2½ oz (65 g) dried
  mushrooms

3 cloves garlic
1 lb (450 g) minced pork
3 tablespoons yellow bean
  paste
1½ tablespoons soya sauce
1 tablespoon chilli sauce
6 tablespoons good stock
2 tablespoons cornflour
  (blended with 6 tablespoons
  water)

Preparation. Boil the noodles for 5 minutes or spaghetti
for 8–10 minutes, then drain. Rinse under running water to
keep separate. Parboil the bean sprouts for 1½ minutes,
then drain. Cut the spring onion and carrots into double
matchstick shreds.

Cooking. Heat the oil in a large frying pan. Add the
mushrooms, garlic and minced pork and stir-fry over
medium heat for 5 minutes. Add the yellow bean sauce, soya
sauce and chilli sauce. Turn and stir-fry them together for 3
minutes. Add the stock and turn and mix the contents until
bubbling hot and well blended. Reduce the heat to low and
simmer gently for 5–6 minutes. Add the blended cornflour
and stir until the sauce has thickened.

Serving. Pour a kettleful of boiling water through the noodles or spaghetti. Drain, and while still hot, place on a well-heated, deep serving dish, on top of a bed of bean sprouts. Arrange the shredded vegetables attractively on top, leaving a space in the centre, and pour the meat sauce into this space. The diners toss the ingredients together before serving themselves.

One of the attractions of this dish is the contrast of the richness of the meat sauce with the fresh crunchiness of the vegetables all piled on top of the hot succulent noodles.

Egg flower soup with tomatoes

Preparation: 2–3 minutes   Cooking: 3–4 minutes

---

1 egg
2 spring onions
3 medium-sized tomatoes
1½ pints (900 ml) good stock

1 chicken stock cube
salt and pepper to taste
1 teaspoon sesame oil

Preparation. Beat the egg lightly in a bowl. Coarsely chop the spring onions and cut each tomato into 6 wedges.

Cooking. Bring the stock to the boil and add the crumbled stock cube. Add the tomatoes, stir and adjust seasoning for salt and pepper. Pour the beaten egg in a narrow stream into the pan, along the prongs of a fork, trailing it over the surface of the soup. When the egg has set, sprinkle the top of the soup with chopped spring onions and sesame oil.

Serving. The soup can either be served in individual bowls or in a large soup tureen for the diners to help themselves from. It acts as a useful 'lubricant' when the noodle dish is not accompanied by a beverage.

MENU B

FOR 4 PEOPLE

Pork sauce noodles

Preparation: 6–7 minutes   Cooking: 1½ hours

The 'sauce noodle' is usually a self-contained dish, where the meat, noodles and vegetables are all cooked together. It is often served in a large soup bowl or in a pot, hence it is often called Pot Noodles. Because during the last phase of the cooking all the ingredients are cooked together, the flavour of the meat permeates into the noodles, while the vegetables retain much of their crunchiness as they are added only towards the end of the cooking. The usual procedure in cooking 'sauce noodles' is to prepare and cook the meat first, followed by the stock and noodles and finally the vegetables. In fact, it is only the meat which requires somewhat lengthy cooking. However, you can use ready cooked meat (usually 'red-cooked' which means it has been braised in soya sauce) in which case the rest of the cooking should not take much more than 10 minutes (if you use Chinese noodles rather than spaghetti). This recipe uses fresh meat.

1¼ lb (500 g) belly of pork
2 slices root ginger
4 tablespoons soya sauce
1 tablespoon sugar
1¼ lb (500 g) Chinese noodles
   or spaghetti
¼ lb (100 g) broccoli
1 medium aubergine

1 pint (600 ml) good stock
1 chicken stock cube
salt and pepper to taste
2 tablespoons cornflour
   (blended with 6 tablespoons
   water)
3 tablespoons red wine

Preparation. Cut the pork into about 20 pieces. Parboil

in boiling water for 5–6 minutes, then drain. Break up the broccoli and cut the aubergine into triple matchstick strips.

Cooking. Place the pork pieces in a large casserole, add the ginger, soya sauce, sugar and ¾ pint (450 ml) water. Bring to the boil, cover and cook in a preheated oven at 190°C, 375°F, gas mark 5 for 1¼ hours, turning the contents over every 30 minutes. Meanwhile, boil and drain the noodles (Chinese noodles for 5 minutes and spaghetti for 8–10 minutes). When the meat is ready, remove the casserole from the oven and place it on top of the cooker. Add the stock and crumbled stock cube to the casserole, followed by the vegetables and noodles. Bring to the boil, then simmer gently for 5 minutes. Adjust the seasoning. Add the blended cornflour and the wine, stirring well. Bring to the boil, then simmer gently for 4 minutes.

Serving. This hearty dish should be brought to the table in the casserole for the diners to help themselves. As it is a self-contained dish, it requires no side dish.

MENU C

FOR 3–4 PEOPLE

Fried noodles (chow mein) with shredded pork and vegetable topping

---

Preparation: 10–20 minutes   Cooking: 8 minutes

¾ lb (350 g) lean pork
2 spring onions
salt and pepper to taste
1 lb (450 g) Chinese noodles or spaghetti
4 tablespoons vegetable oil

¼ lb (100 g) bean sprouts
3 tablespoons soya sauce
1½ teaspoons brown sugar
3 tablespoons good stock

Preparation. Cut pork with a sharp knife into matchstick shreds and rub with salt and pepper. Cut the spring onions into 2 inch (5 cm) pieces. Parboil the noodles for 4–5 minutes or the spaghetti for 8–10 minutes and drain.

Cooking. Heat the oil in a frying pan. Add the pork and stir-fry over high heat for 2 minutes. Add the spring onions and bean sprouts and continue to stir-fry for 2 minutes. Add the soya sauce, sugar and stock. Turn and stir together for 1½ minutes then remove ¾ of the mixture and put aside. Add the noodles to mix with the remaining sauce and ingredients in the pan. Stir and toss them together over medium heat for 3 minutes, then transfer to a serving dish.

Serving. Add the reserved pork and vegetables to a frying pan and stir-fry over high heat for 1 minute. Pour the contents over the noodles as a topping.

MENU D

Ham and chicken sauce noodles with soya egg

Preparation: 10 minutes   Cooking: 20 minutes

Ham and chicken pot-cooked sauce noodles with soya egg is often served as a welcoming dish for a Chinese birthday party, because we Chinese believe that eggs represent reproduction and continuity.

Soya eggs are produced very simply by turning and heating hard-boiled eggs in a pan filled with, say, ¼ pint (150 ml) of soya sauce. When hard-boiled eggs are cooked in soya sauce, they will take on a rich deep brown colour in a matter of minutes. Because of the flavour imparted by the soya sauce, we find 'soya eggs' a very useful complement to plain bulk foods, especially rice; but in this case they are eaten with noodles and one egg is added whole to a bowl of noodles. The diner takes a bite at the egg with every few mouthfuls of noodles mixed with shredded chicken, ham, and vegetables. The egg provides a somewhat different flavour and texture from all the other ingredients in the bowl.

¼ lb (100 g) ham
½ lb (225 g) cooked chicken
  breast meat
3 spring onions
1 lb (450 g) Chinese noodles or
  spaghetti
4 soya eggs

2 pints (1.2 litres) good stock
2 chicken stock cubes
salt and pepper to taste
2 tablespoons cornflour
  (blended in 6 tablespoons
  water)
2 tablespoons light soya sauce

Preparation. Cut the ham and chicken into matchstick shreds. Cut the spring onions into coarse shavings.

134

Cooking. Boil the noodles for 4–5 minutes or spaghetti for 8–10 minutes and drain. Prepare the soya eggs (as directed above). Heat the stock in a saucepan. When it boils, stir and add the crumbled stock cubes, then adjust the seasoning with salt and pepper. Stir in the blended cornflour to thicken. Add the noodles and soya sauce and simmer for 4 minutes.

Serving. Divide the noodles and sauce equally into 4 serving bowls. Place a soya egg on top of the noodles in each of the bowls. Place bundles of shredded ham and chicken (separately) around the egg. Sprinkle the contents of the bowls with spring onion shavings and serve.

The contrast between the colour and shape of the egg with the pink of the ham, the white of the chicken and green of the spring onion, makes a particularly decorative and interesting dish. Once again this is a self-contained dish which requires nothing else to go with it.

MENU E

FOR 3–4 PEOPLE

Fish-head pot-cooked noodles with oyster and spring onions

Preparation: 30 minutes   Cooking: 45 minutes

Although seldom used in the West, fish-heads are often eaten in China. They are regarded as a delicacy when cooked with care, especially if a good cut can be obtained from the fishmonger, when over an inch or two (2.5–5 cm) of the fish meat is chopped off to be included with the head. Well seasoned and flavoured, this makes an extremely delicious dish, which benefits from the addition of stock and noodles to the pot during the last 5–6 minutes of cooking.

1 large (2 lbs (1 kg)) fish-head (salmon, salmon trout, sea-bream, sea-bass, halibut, pike etc).
1 lb (450 g) Chinese noodles or spaghetti

For parboiling
1½ tablespoons salt
6 slices root ginger

For sauce and dressing
3 oz (75 g) dried mushrooms
4 rashers bacon
¼ lb (100 g) Chinese 'snow pickles' (or chutney)

2 tablespoons Chinese salted black beans
2 medium onions
3 spring onions
2 cloves garlic
4 tablespoons vegetable oil
1 tablespoon sugar
3 tablespoons dark soya sauce
¼ pint (150 ml) good stock, plus 1 pint (600 ml) stock and 1½ chicken stock cubes for noodles
4 tablespoons dry sherry
1¼ tablespoons cornflour (blended with 3 tablespoons water)

Preparation. Soak the dried mushrooms in hot water for

136

20 minutes and drain (remove any hard stems, if necessary). Boil the salt and ginger in 1½ pints (900 ml) water for 3 minutes. Add the fish head (or heads) to it for 4 minutes and drain. Cut the bacon across lean and fat into matchstick shreds. Chop the pickles coarsely. Soak the black beans in warm water for 2 minutes and drain. Cut the onions into thin slices and spring onions into ½ inch (1 cm) slices. Parboil the noodles for 3 minutes or spaghetti for 5 minutes and drain.

Cooking. Heat the oil in a large casserole. Add the onion slices and bacon and stir-fry for 2 minutes. Add the mushrooms, pickles and black beans and stir-fry all the ingredients together for 2 minutes. Place the fish head in the casserole and spoon the ingredients and hot oil over it. Fry the fish for 2½ minutes on each side. Add the sugar, soya sauce, stock and half the sherry. Bring to the boil and turn the fish head in the sauce several times. Cover and cook over low heat for 15 minutes, turning the fish head over once. Remove the lid and reduce the sauce in the casserole to less than a quarter of its original volume by cooking over high heat (if necessary). Add the stock, sprinkled with crumbled stock cube. Bring to the boil again, then thicken by stirring in the blended cornflour. Add the noodles and continue cooking over low heat for 5 minutes. Stir the noodles and fish together thoroughly.

Serving. Sprinkle the contents of the casserole with spring onion and serve by bringing the casserole to the table. This should make a hearty, delicious and substantial dish. Since fish heads are still very inexpensive on the Western market (they can occasionally be obtained free), this should also be a very inexpensive dish to produce. As the fish bones from the fish heads are seldom pointed, they can be quite easily removed and should present less of a threat to the noodle-eater than more expensive cuts of fish. It is a dish well worth trying.

MENU F

FOR 4 PEOPLE

Pot-cooked noodles with oyster and spring onions
Basic chow mein poached in stock with Chinese cabbage
Tomato and courgette soup with bean curd

Pot-cooked noodles with oyster and spring onions

Preparation: 10 minutes   Cooking: 20 minutes

1 lb (450 g) Chinese noodles (or spaghetti)
4 spring onions
4 slices root ginger
3 teaspoons vegetable oil
salt and pepper to taste
¼ lb (100 g) minced pork

2 tablespoons light soya sauce
¼ pint (150 ml) good stock
1 chicken stock cube
¼ pint (150 ml) red or white wine
12 medium oysters
¾ teaspoon sesame oil

Preparation. Parboil the noodles for 3 minutes and drain. If using spaghetti, cook for 5 minutes and drain. Rinse the noodles or spaghetti under running water. Cut spring onions into 1½ inch (4 cm) pieces. Keep the white and green pieces separate. Coarsely chop the ginger.

Cooking. Heat the oil in a frying pan. Add the ginger, white part of the spring onions, salt and minced pork. Stir together over medium heat for 3 minutes. Add pepper, soya sauce, stock, chicken stock cube and wine. Increase the heat and bring to the boil. Stir once, reduce the heat and leave to cook gently for 5–6 minutes. Prise open the oysters over the pan, allowing the oyster liquor to drip into the pan as each oyster is detached (with the aid of a knife) and dropped into it. When all the oysters have been opened and dropped into the pan stir the contents around a few times. Place the noodles in a casserole and pour over the contents of the frying pan. Place over a low heat and simmer gently for 5–6 minutes. Sprinkle with the green parts of the spring onions, and sesame oil.

Serving. Serve by bringing the casserole to the table for the diners to help themselves.

Basic chow mein poached in stock with Chinese cabbage

Preparation: 30 minutes   Cooking: 8 minutes

The basic Chinese technique in cooking chow mein is first of all to stir-fry dried, salty or strong-tasting ingredients in a small amount of oil. When their flavours have been released into the oil, the flavoured oil is then used to turn and stir the noodles in. It is only afterwards that the other flavourings (e.g. soya sauce, stock, wine etc.) are added. In the final phase of cooking the fresh ingredients, such as prawns and other seafoods and chopped vegetables are freshly cooked and placed as a garnish on top of the noodles.

4–5 large Chinese dried
  mushrooms
1½ tablespoons dried shrimps
1½ lbs (750 g) Chinese
  noodles or spaghetti
2 medium onions
2 cloves garlic
1 tablespoon Chinese 'winter
  pickle' (or chutney)

3 rashers bacon
4 tablespoons vegetable oil
1 teaspoon salt
2 tablespoons dark soya sauce
1½ tablespoons light soya
  sauce
For garnish and dressing
3 oz (75 g) chicken breast meat
2 slices root ginger
3 spring onions

139

1½ tablespoons vegetable oil
¼ lb (100 g) fresh or frozen
  shrimps
3 tablespoons good stock
2 tablespoons dry sherry

Preparation. Soak the mushrooms and dried shrimps in 6 tablespoons of boiling water for 30 minutes (retain the soaking water). Parboil the noodles for 3 minutes, or spaghetti for 5 minutes and drain. Rinse them under running water to keep separate. Thinly slice the onion and garlic. Chop the pickles coarsely. Cut the chicken and ginger into matchstick shreds and the spring onions into 1 inch (2.5 cm) sections. Cut the bacon into matchsticks, having removed the rind.

Cooking. Heat the oil in a large frying pan. Add the bacon, pickles, garlic, soaked dried shrimps, salt and mushrooms and stir-fry for 3–4 minutes. Add the noodles, stirring well to take on a savoury coating from the 'flavoured oil'. Sprinkle the noodles with soya sauce and shrimp and mushroom water. Leave to cook gently, turning every 30 seconds until the noodles have heated through thoroughly. Meanwhile, make the garnish and dressing. In a small frying pan heat the oil and stock over high heat. When they come to a rolling boil add the shrimps and other ingredients. Stir-fry over high heat for 1½ minutes. Place on top of the noodles as a garnish and allow the sauce to seep down through the noodles to enhance their flavour.

Serving. Transfer the contents of the pan to a large serving dish and allow the diners to help themselves. As this is a comparatively dry dish, it is useful to have a bowl of soup to go with it.

Tomato and courgette soup with bean curd

Preparation: 4 minutes   Cooking: 5 minutes

This is a quick and simple soup which can be readily prepared with the minimum of trouble. It is a useful supplement to the Chow Mein, providing both a liquid element to the meal as well as some additional nutritional value.

2 medium courgettes
4 medium tomatoes
1 cake bean curd
2 teaspoons dried shrimps
1½ pints (900 ml) good stock

1 chicken stock cube
salt and pepper to taste
1½ tablespoons light soya
   sauce
1½ teaspoons sesame oil

Preparation. Cut the courgettes into thin slices, and the tomatoes into quarters. Cut the bean curd into 12 pieces.

Cooking. Place the dried shrimps in a saucepan, pour in the stock and bring to the boil. Add the courgettes, tomatoes and crumbled stock cube. Bring to the boil again, then simmer gently for 5 minutes. Adjust the seasoning with salt and pepper. Add the bean curd and soya sauce and heat, stirring, for 2–3 minutes. Sprinkle with sesame oil.

Serving. Serve in a large soup tureen for the diners to help themselves. This is a light soup, but its natural vegetable flavour makes it a welcome complement to the noodles.

FISH AND SEAFOOD

In Chinese cooking, fish and seafood (like the best cuts of meats) are usually very quickly cooked, in order that they may retain their natural quality and flavour. They are normally cooked by steaming or quick shallow-frying (as opposed to quick stir-frying) owing to the fact that fish may break up into unsightly pieces if vigorously stirred and tossed. The one distinguishing ingredient which we Chinese use in fish and seafood cookery is ginger; this is often used in conjunction with garlic and onion (or spring onion). When ginger is used, or when all of these strong-tasting foods are used in conjunction with each other, they have the ability to counteract any 'fishiness' in fish and seafoods, thus making them much more acceptable to the palate. In applying these strong-tasting vegetables to fish in steaming, the vegetables are simply cut and piled on the fish in the cooking process, along with one or two dried or salted ingredients such as dried shrimps, mushrooms, or salted meats such as bacon.

When frying fish, the ginger and vegetables are usually fried in the oil first in order to impregnate the oil with their flavours. The flavoured oil is then used to fry the fish, or to make a sauce in which the fish is coated. Since shrimps and prawns are of a size which is just right for stir-frying, they are usually cooked in that way. The larger crustaceans require a short period of braising with wine or stock after an initial frying or stir-frying, to complete their cooking. In these latter cases, there is often a good amount of extremely tasty sauce created as a by-product. The sauce can be applied to bulk food (rice or noodles) or vegetables, with the most salutary effect. One notices here the extreme difference

143

between the Chinese concept of sauces and sauce-making as compared with the French. The French create sauces to apply to meats, fish and seafoods. We Chinese produce sauces as by-products in the cooking of these foods. Consequently the Chinese sauces, some of them supreme in quality and flavour, are often nameless, mainly because the focus is on the production of the whole dish and the cooking of the principal foods, rather than on the production of any sauce. Hence there may well be many more sauces in the Chinese cuisine than in the French – they run into scores of hundreds – but few people can recall the name of any of them!

MENU A

FOR 4 PEOPLE

*Home-cooked soya braised fish
Steaks with ginger and spring onion
Steamed vegetable rice with Brussels
sprouts*

Home-cooked soya braised fish steaks with ginger and spring onion

Preparation: 6 minutes   Cooking: 6 minutes

1½ lbs (750 g) fish steaks (cod, haddock, halibut, bream or turbot)
1½ teaspoons salt
pepper to taste
1½ tablespoons dark soya sauce
5 tablespoons vegetable oil

For the sauce
3 slices root ginger
1 medium onion
3 spring onions
2½ tablespoons light soya sauce
2½ teaspoons sugar
2½ tablespoons good stock
2½ tablespoons dry sherry

Preparation. Cut the fish into 8 regular-sized pieces. Rub with salt, pepper, soya sauce and 2 teaspoons of the oil. Shred the ginger, thinly slice the onion, and cut the spring onions into 1 inch (2.5 cm) lengths.

Cooking. Heat the remaining oil in a medium frying pan. Spread out the fish in the pan. Fry for 2 minutes, turning once and basting continuously with oil. Remove the fish and set aside to drain. Add the onion and ginger and stir-fry in the remaining oil for 1½ minutes. Add the soya sauce, sugar, stock and sherry and stir-fry for 1 minute, or until the liquid has reduced by half. Return the fish to the pan and sprinkle

145

with spring onions. Turn the fish gently, to cook on all sides in the sauce over low heat for 2 minutes. By this time the surface of the fish will have turned a deep brown in colour and become impregnated with the taste of ginger and sugar, as well as the saltiness of the soya sauce. These contrast well with the juicy savouriness of the white meat of the fish underneath.

Serving. Fish cooked in this way is an excellent complement to plain, boiled rice, especially when the fish gravy and spring onion in which it has been fried and cooked are added to the rice. Many connoisseurs of Chinese home-cooking think that this simply cooked dish of fish is possessed of a quality of flavour which few meat dishes are able to match.

Steamed vegetable rice with Brussels sprouts

Preparation: 8 minutes   Cooking: 12 minutes

1 lb (450 g) rice	2 tablespoons vegetable oil
¾ lb (350 g) Brussels sprouts	1½ teaspoons salt

Preparation. Boil the rice gently in its own volume of water for 8 minutes. Remove from the heat. Clean and trim the sprouts, removing any discoloured leaves and tougher parts of the stem. Cut each sprout in half (or large ones into quarters). Heat the oil in a small frying pan. Add the sprouts, sprinkle with salt and stir over high heat for 1 minute.

Cooking. Divide the sprouts between 4 large heatproof rice bowls or basins and put the rice on top. Place the bowls in a steamer and steam for 12 minutes. Serve the rice in the bowls, one for each diner. This is excellent served with a meat dish or a fish dish, especially when there are no other dishes served to make up the meal. The presence of vegetables in some quantity in the rice helps to achieve a good balance to the meal, not only nutritionally, but also in colour; the deep brown of the fish, white of the rice and the bright green of the sprouts, makes an attractive combination.

MENU B

FOR 4 PEOPLE

Soya braised fish steak with minced pork, pickles and dried mushrooms
Steamed vegetable rice with courgettes and carrots

Soya braised fish steak with minced pork, pickles and dried mushrooms

Preparation: 8 minutes   Soaking: 30 minutes
Cooking: 15 minutes

This is a variation of the previous recipe. It is more often served at party meals than in home cooking. By adding pork, pickle and mushrooms in the sauce preparation, a more elaborate dish is created, and because the fish is cooked for longer a delicious sauce is produced.

1½ lb (750 g) fish steaks (cod, haddock, halibut, bream or turbot)
2 teaspoons salt
pepper to taste
1½ tablespoons dark soya sauce
5 tablespoons vegetable oil

For the sauce
2 oz (50 g) dried mushrooms
1 medium onion
3 spring onions
3 slices root ginger
2 oz (50 g) Chinese green 'snow pickle' (or gherkins)
2 tablespoons vegetable oil
½ lb (225 g) minced pork
2 tablespoons light soya sauce
1½ tablespoons yellow bean sauce
1½ tablespoons chilli sauce
6 tablespoons good stock
3 tablespoons dry sherry
1 tablespoon sugar
1 chicken stock cube

Preparation. Soak the mushrooms in half a bowl of boiling

148

water for 30 minutes. Drain and shred (having discarded the stems). Reserve 3 tablespoons of the soaking water. Cut the fish into 8 regular pieces. Rub evenly with the salt, pepper, soya sauce and 2 teaspoons of the vegetable oil. Cut the onion into thin slices and the spring onion into 1 inch (2.5 cm) lengths. Shred the ginger and coarsely chop the pickles.

Cooking. Heat the remaining oil in a medium frying pan. Add the fish, spreading out the pieces in the pan. Cook for 2 minutes, turning once and basting frequently. Remove the fish and put aside to drain.

Pour the oil for the sauce into the pan. Add the onion, ginger and shredded dried mushrooms and stir-fry over high heat for 1½ minutes. Add the pork, sprinkle with salt and continue to turn and stir-fry for the next 2½ minutes. Pour in the soya sauce, yellow bean sauce, chilli sauce, stock, sherry, sugar and mushroom water. Cook over medium heat for 2 minutes, stirring. Return the pieces of fish to the centre of the pan. Baste and cover them with the sauce ingredients already in the pan. Cover and cook over low heat for 8 minutes.

Serving. Transfer the fish pieces to a deep serving dish. Sprinkle the contents of the pan with spring onion, crumbled stock cube and 6 tablespoons water, then bring to a vigorous boil. Stir quickly and when the liquid in the pan has been reduced by half pour all the sauce over the fish pieces in the serving dish.

Steamed vegetable rice with courgettes and carrots

Preparation: 8 minutes   Cooking: 12 minutes

This is a very similar dish and cooked in the same manner as the 'vegetable rice' of the previous menu. The only adjustments are with the vegetables used; courgettes and carrots instead of Brussels sprouts.

1 lb (450 g) rice	1½ teaspoons salt
½ lb (225 g) courgettes	2 tablespoons melted butter
½ lb (225 g) young carrots	

Preparation. Wash the rice and boil in its own volume of water for 8 minutes. Remove from the heat. Clean and cut the courgettes and carrots into 1 inch (2.5 cm) lengths. Parboil them for 1½ minutes, drain and place in 4 large serving bowls. Sprinkle with salt and melted butter while still hot.

Cooking and serving. Put the partly cooked rice on top of the vegetables in the bowls. Place the bowls in a steamer and steam for 12 minutes. Rice and vegetables cooked in this way should be enjoyable to eat with any well-flavoured dish, whether crispy and deep-fried, or saucy and stir-fried. Served with braised fish, the natural bland taste should contrast well with the richness of the fish, pork and sauce.

MENU C

FOR 4 PEOPLE

Baked marinated fish
Stir-fried and sautéed spring cabbage
with onions and mushrooms
Boiled white or brown rice

Baked marinated fish

Preparation: 5 minutes   Cooking: 18 minutes
Seasoning: 15 minutes

1 large rainbow trout (or 2 small trout about 1 lb (450 g) each)	**2½ teaspoons salt**
	pepper to taste
2–3 slices root ginger	**2 tablespoons hoisin sauce**
3 spring onions	**2 tablespoons vegetable oil**

Preparation. Preheat oven to 200°C, 400°F, gas mark 6. Wash and clean the fish thoroughly and pat dry. Finely chop the ginger and cut the spring onions into 1 inch (2.5 cm) lengths. Rub the fish with ginger, salt and pepper, then stuff with the spring onions. Leave to stand for 15 minutes, then rub thoroughly with hoisin sauce and oil, putting a quarter of the sauce and oil into the belly of the fish.

Cooking. Wrap the fish in kitchen foil, place in a roasting tin and bake in a preheated oven at 200°C, 400°F, gas mark 6 for 18 minutes.

Serving. Serve by unwrapping the fish and placing it on a bed of hot boiled rice.

Stir-fried and sautéed spring cabbage with onions and mushrooms

Preparation: 5 minutes   Cooking: 20 minutes

1 spring cabbage (about 1 lb
  (450 g))
2 medium onions
2 rashers bacon
¼ lb (100 g) button
  mushrooms

3 tablespoons vegetable oil
2 tablespoons soya sauce
1½ tablespoons hoisin sauce
  (optional)
½ tablespoon sugar

Preparation. Clean and cut the cabbage into 1½ inch (4 cm) pieces. Cut the onions into thin slices and the bacon into matchstick shreds. Cut the mushrooms into halves or quarters, depending on size.

Cooking. Heat the oil in a casserole, add the bacon and onion and stir-fry for 1½ minutes. Add the spring cabbage and mushrooms. Stir and turn them together quickly over high heat. Add the soya sauce, hoisin sauce and sugar. Stir together for 1 minute, then add 5 tablespoons of water and mix well together. Cover and place in the oven at the same time as the rice.

Boiled white or brown rice

There are many ways of cooking boiled rice; the simplest method is described on page 32. However, since the oven is already on to bake the fish, we might as well use it to cook the rice for this menu. You will need 1 lb (450 g) of rice.

Preparation. Wash, rinse and drain the rice. Place it in a casserole with its own volume of water.

Cooking. As soon as the fish has been placed in the oven to bake, bring the rice quickly to the boil, cover and cook in the oven at the same time as the fish. The fish, rice and vegetables should all be ready at the same time.

Serving. Spread out the rice on a large oval dish and place the fish on top. Serve the vegetables straight from the casserole. The bland, plainly cooked rice should act as an excellent background to the well-flavoured fish, cabbage and slightly sweet sauce.

MENU D

---

*Steamed sea bass with shredded ginger
and spring onion or Cantonese steamed
whole fish
Steamed rice with leeks*

Steamed sea bass with shredded ginger and spring onion

Preparation: 35 minutes   Cooking: 15 minutes

1¼–1¾ lb (500–850 g) fish (sea bass, bream or trout)	1 tablespoon vegetable oil
1½ teaspoons salt and pepper	3 slices root ginger
1½ tablespoons light soya	3 spring onions
	1½ tablespoons sherry

Preparation. Clean and chop the fish through the bone into 2 inch (5 cm) sections. Rub the pieces with salt, pepper, soya sauce and oil, then set aside for 30 minutes. Cut the ginger and spring onions into matchstick pieces.

Cooking. Place the fish pieces in a heatproof dish. Arrange the shredded ginger and spring onions on top of them. Sprinkle with sherry. Place the dish in a steamer and steam vigorously for 15 minutes.

Serving. Bring the dish straight to the table. There should be two pieces of fish for each person and the sauce from the fish is delicious when eaten with boiled rice.

Cantonese steamed whole fish

Preparation: 30 minutes   Cooking: 20 minutes

1 large fish (sea bass, salmon trout or carp) about 1½ lbs (750g)
4 Chinese dried mushrooms
2 tablespoons dried shrimps
2½ teaspoons salt and pepper to taste

3 slices root ginger
8 spring onions
3 tablespoons light soya sauce
2 tablespoons dry sherry
4 tablespoons vegetable oil
2 rashers of bacon

Preparation. Soak the dried shrimps and dried mushrooms for 20 minutes in a bowl of hot water. Discard the mushroom stalks and slice the caps into strips. Slice the bacon into thin strips. Wash and clean the fish inside and out. Rub it thoroughly with salt and pepper and 1 tablespoon of the oil. Cut the ginger into matchstick shreds and 2 of the spring onions into 1½ inch (4 cm) lengths. Stuff the fish with half the ginger and the spring onions and place it on a heatproof oval dish. Sprinkle the shrimps over the top of the fish, drape it with the strips of bacon and mushrooms and sprinkle with pepper.

Cooking. Put the dish in a steamer and steam vigorously for 18–20 minutes. Remove the fish from the steamer and pour away half the condensed liquid in the dish. Arrange the remaining ginger over the length of the fish and pour over the soya sauce and sherry. Heat the oil in a small saucepan until very hot. Pour it in a thin stream on top of the fish and decorate the dish with whole spring onions and dried mushrooms. This is acclaimed as one of the great fish dishes of the world.

Steamed rice with leeks

Preparation: 15 minutes   Cooking: 20 minutes

1 lb (450 g) brown rice
1 tablespoon dried shrimps
½ lb (225 g) young leeks

1½ tablespoons soya sauce
1½ tablespoons vegetable oil
1 tablespoon wine vinegar

Preparation. Boil the brown rice in ample water for 15 minutes and drain. Meanwhile, soak dried shrimps for 15 minutes and drain. Clean and cut the leeks slantwise into 1½ inch (4 cm) lengths. Divide the leeks between 4 large heatproof rice bowls or basins. Sprinkle with dried shrimps, soya sauce, oil and vinegar and divide the rice between the bowls.

Cooking. Place the bowls in the steamer and steam for the same length of time as the fish (18–20 minutes).

Serving. The 4 bowls of rice and leeks are brought steaming to the table, 1 bowl for each diner. The large oval dish of steaming fish is placed in the centre for the gathering to help themselves. The diners will take pieces of fish and spoonfuls of sauce from the centre dish and place or pour them on the rice. Occasionally they will dig up the leeks from the bottom of their rice bowls to mix and eat with the ingredients piled on top. Rice and vegetables steamed in this way usually retain their heat for a good length of time.

MENU E

---

*Foochow crab-rice with ginger, leeks
and garlic
Mussels, bean curd and mushroom soup*

Foochow crab-rice with ginger, leeks and garlic

Preparation: 30 minutes   Cooking: 20 minutes

This was one of my favourite dishes when I was a teenager
in my hometown in Foochow. Crab-rice is a self-contained
dish, like Paella, which can be eaten without resorting to any
other supplementary dishes. It is a dish for the hungry –
when turned out from the basin in which it has been cooked,
it becomes a mountain of colourful foods – and, for those
who do not mind picking the meat out of the shells, a real
feast. Foochow is a seaport where seafoods abound, but this
is one of the rare cases where a seafood is actually cooked
with rice.

2 large or 3 medium freshly
  cooked crabs (about 3 lbs
  (1.25 kg))
1 lb (450 g) rice
½ lb (225 g) young leeks
1 teaspoon salt
1½ oz (40 g) butter

For the sauce
3 slices root ginger
3 cloves garlic
2 spring onions
4 tablespoons soya sauce
2 tablespoons wine vinegar
2 tablespoons dry sherry
2 tablespoons vegetable oil
2 teaspoons sesame oil

Preparation. Prepare the sauce by chopping the ginger,
garlic and spring onion coarsely and placing in a bowl with

157

the soya sauce, vinegar, sherry, oil and sesame oil. Clean and cut the leeks slantwise into 1 inch (2.5 cm) lengths.

Place the crabs upside down and chop each in half right through the body and top shell. Further chop each half of the body into 3 pieces. Place the crab pieces in a large bowl and pour over the prepared sauce. Turn them over several times, so that each piece of crab is well sauced. Wash the rice and boil it in its own volume of water for 8 minutes and remove from the heat.

Cooking. Place the leeks in a large heatproof basin and sprinkle with salt and melted butter. Pack half the part-cooked rice on top of the leeks. Place half of the marinated pieces of crab on top of the rice. Cover with the remainder of the rice and spread the rest of the crabs on top. Sprinkle over the rest of the marinade. Place the basin in a steamer and steam vigorously for 15 minutes.

Serving. Remove the basin from the steamer and turn the contents out on to a large heated serving dish. The mound of extremely savoury food may weigh 5–6 lbs (2¼–2¾ kg) which should provide plenty for the diners to help themselves from. In addition, 1 or 2 bowls of dip-sauce may be provided on the table by mixing 2 tablespoons chilli sauce with 4 tablespoons soya sauce, for the diners to dip their crab pieces into if they like their food to be highly spiced.

Mussels, bean curd and mushroom soup

Preparation: 10 minutes   Soaking: 20 minutes
Cooking: 20 minutes

2 pints (1.2 litres) fresh
  mussels
2 oz (50 g) smoked pork or
  ham
6 medium Chinese dried
  mushrooms (or 2 oz (50 g)
  any dried mushrooms)

3 spring onions
2 cakes bean curd
2 pints (1.2 litres) good stock
3 slices root ginger
(blended with 6 tablespoons
  water)
3 tablespoons dry sherry

1½ chicken stock cubes   2 tablespoons cornflour
1½ teaspoons salt
pepper to taste

Preparation. Brush and clean the mussels individually and thoroughly under running water. Coarsely chop the smoked pork or ham. Meanwhile, soak the dried mushrooms in hot water for 20 minutes. Remove the stems and cut the caps into shreds. Cut the spring onions into 1 inch (2.5 cm) lengths. Plunge the mussels into a pan of boiling water to parboil for 1½ minutes and drain. Cut each piece of bean curd into 20–24 pieces.

Cooking. Heat the stock in a saucepan. Add ginger, chopped pork or ham and shredded mushrooms. Remove the mussels from their shells and drop them into the stock, together with any mussel water from the shells. Add the crumbled stock cubes. Bring the contents to the boil, then reduce the heat to low and simmer gently for 10 minutes. Stir in the bean curd and adjust the seasoning with salt and pepper. When the contents reboil, stir in the blended cornflour and sprinkle with spring onion shavings and dry sherry.

Serving. This nutritious mussel soup is delicious when eaten with Crab-Rice and should be a memorable experience for anyone who has a liking for seafoods.

MENU F

Stir-fry 'three sea flavours' in black bean sauce or Prawns in two textures Steamed rice with lettuce and green peas

Stir-fry 'three sea flavours' in black bean sauce

Preparation: 10 minutes   Cooking: 6 minutes

½ lb (225 g) prawns (fresh or frozen)
5 oz (150 g) scallop meat (fresh or frozen)
½ lb (225 g) squid (fresh or frozen)
1 teaspoon salt
pepper to taste
1 tablespoon finely chopped root ginger

4 tablespoons vegetable oil
2 tablespoons salted black beans
1 medium onion
1 medium pepper (red or green)
1 tablespoon light soya sauce
1½ tablespoons dry sherry
2 tablespoons good stock

Preparation. Thaw the seafood (if frozen). Clean and cut the squid into ½ × 1½ inch (1 × 4 cm) pieces. Rub the squid, prawns and scallops with salt, pepper, ginger and ½ tablespoon of the oil. Meanwhile, soak the black beans in water for 5 minutes and drain. Cut the onions and pepper into thin slices.

Cooking. Heat the remaining oil in a frying pan. Add the onion and stir-fry for 1½ minutes. Add the black beans and mix and mash with the onions and oil. Add all the seafoods and turn them in the mixture over high heat for 2 minutes.

Pour in the soya sauce, sherry and stock and add the peppers. Stir and turn vigorously for 1 minute and serve.

Serving. This is a salty dish with an unusual 'earthy' flavour, which is very acceptable to most people. It is best eaten with quantities of plain-cooked rice and vegetables.

Prawns in two textures

Preparation: 15 minutes   Cooking: 6–7 minutes

---

20 large prawns	pepper to taste
1 egg	2 cloves garlic
5 tablespoons plain flour	oil for deep-frying
1½ tablespoons self-raising flour	2 spring onions
1½ tablespoons cornflour	1½ tablespoons good stock
1½ teaspoons salt	2 teaspoons light soya sauce
	1½ tablespoons dry sherry

Preparation. Clean and remove the shells of 10 of the prawns. Remove the shells of the remaining 10 only up to the tails (the tails are left on for colour and convenience of handling). Beat the egg and blend in a mixing bowl with the flours into a smooth batter. Dip the prawns with tails in the batter, up to the tails. Sprinkle and rub the remaining prawns with salt, pepper, and 2 teaspoons of oil. Crush the garlic, and coarsely chop the spring onions.

Cooking. Heat the oil in the deep-fryer. When the oil is hot (when a crumb will sizzle when dropped in it) lower the battered prawns into the oil one at a time and deep-fry for 2½ minutes. Remove and drain on absorbent paper. Heat 4 tablespoons oil in a wok or frying-pan. Add the chopped spring onion and garlic. Stir a few times over medium heat, then add the remaining prawns and stir-fry for ¾ minute. Add the stock, soya sauce and sherry. Turn the heat high, and stir for 1 minute.

Serving. Turn the contents of the pan into the centre of a large round serving dish. Arrange the deep-fried prawns in a circle around them with their tails pointing outwards for convenience of handling. This is an attractive dish which will impress guests at parties.

Steamed rice with lettuce and green peas

Preparation: 15 minutes   Cooking: 15 minutes

1 lb (450 g) brown rice
¾ lb (350 g) lettuce
½ lb (225 g) green peas (fresh
   or frozen)
3 oz (75 g) butter

Preparation. Add the rice to a pan of boiling water, boil for 15 minutes and drain. Tear the lettuce leaves into approximately 2 × 3 inch (5 × 7.5 cm) pieces. Line 4 large heatproof rice bowls or basins with the lettuce leaves. Divide the peas into 4 portions and put them on top of the lettuce leaves. Place a dollop of butter on top of the vegetables in each of the bowls.

Cooking. While still hot, put the rice on top of the vegetables in the bowls. Place the bowls in a steamer and steam vigorously for 15 minutes.

MENU G

FOR 4 PEOPLE

The chiang-nan or 'south of the river' shrimps and prawn noodles (a snack dish)

Preparation: 6 minutes   Soaking: 30 minutes
Cooking: 8 minutes

---

2 tablespoons dried shrimps
8 medium Chinese dried
  mushrooms
10 oz (275 g) peeled shrimps
  (fresh or frozen)
8 oz (225 g) large peeled
  prawns (fresh or frozen)
1½ teaspoons salt
pepper to taste
1 tablespoon finely chopped
  root ginger

4 tablespoons vegetable oil
4 sticks celery
6 spring onions
1½ lb (750 g) rice-flour
  noodles
2 tablespoons light soya sauce
2 tablespoons shrimp sauce
3 tablespoons dry sherry
3 tablespoons good stock
1½ oz (40 g) butter

Preparation. Soak the dried shrimps and mushrooms in a bowl of boiling water for 30 minutes and drain. Shred the mushrooms caps, having removed the stems. Retain the mushroom water. Rub the shrimps and prawns with salt, pepper, ginger and a little of the oil. Clean and cut the celery into triple matchstick shreds and the spring onions into 2 inch (5 cm) lengths. Parboil the noodles for 4 minutes and drain, then rinse under running water to keep separate.

Cooking. Heat the remaining oil in a large frying pan. Add the dried shrimps, dried mushrooms and half the spring onion (the white part) and stir-fry over medium heat for 1½ minutes. Add 6 tablespoons of the shrimp/mushroom

163

water, increase the heat to high and continue to stir-fry for 1 minute. Add the fresh shrimps and celery. Stir and turn them over in the bubbling sauce for 1½ minutes. Add the noodles and mix with the sauce, celery, shrimps, dried shrimps and dried mushrooms. In no time the noodles will have picked up the flavours from all these ingredients. Add 2–3 teaspoons soya sauce, shrimp sauce, sherry and stock. Turn the contents over several times so that the ingredients will heat through and be evenly mixed.

Heat the butter in a small frying pan. When it has melted add the remaining spring onions, soya sauce, shrimp sauce, stock and sherry. When the mixture bubbles, add the prawns and stir together for 1½ minutes. Arrange the noodles on a heated serving dish and pour the seafood mixture on top.

Serving. This large dish of noodles provides an excellent, highly appetizing snack for high-tea or for anyone who has had too long to wait for a late dinner or supper.

VEGETABLES

Vegetables abound in China. Indeed, Western people who visit China for the first time may easily gain the impression that the Chinese are largely vegetarian. Of ten dishes served on the table three are usually purely vegetable dishes, and another three part-vegetable dishes. With Chinese food, because of the tradition of mixing and blending of ingredients and materials, whether a dish is a meat or a vegetable one is largely a matter of degree. It depends on which of the ingredients predominate; if meat and meat flavour predominate, it will be called a meat dish; if vegetables constitute more than 80 per cent of a dish, then the dish is likely to be considered a vegetable dish. Even with that percentage, the dish may still be considered a meat dish or a meat-and-vegetable dish. Since in most cases meat is deemed more valuable, or at least more expensive, than vegetables, it is often given priority in the christening of a dish.

In the Chinese way of stir-frying vegetables, they are treated in much the same manner as when making a Western salad. The only difference is that the Chinese way is to toss the vegetables in hot oil rather than cold.

Stir-fried Chinese vegetable dishes are the easiest vegetable dishes for Westerners to appreciate, since the idea of cooking vegetables lightly and keeping them crisp appeals to anyone interested in eating well and in a healthy manner.

But there are other ways of cooking vegetables which make them even more important and appetizing to the Chinese, which result in their eating more vegetables than the average Westerner. One of these ways is to braise or sauté them for a matter of 15–25 minutes. When cooked in this way, the vegetables are tenderized by the longer cooking, made more delicious by the addition of meat broth, gravy, and soya ingredients and also much smoother and more sumptuous by the use of oil. These varied methods of cooking and flavouring often result in the vegetables assuming something of the quality of meat, thus encouraging large quantities of them to be eaten. There are in the Chinese repertoire many vegetable stews which are of great interest to big rice-eaters, as they can often make up something of the gap left by the shortage of meat. One of the most popularly used flavourings is dried shrimps, often supplemented by dried mushrooms and if necessary further reinforced by the inclusion of a small amount of salted meat (e.g. bacon, salt beef etc.) These are all used in very small quantities together with a little stock. When soya sauce is added during the cooking, the dish is called 'red-cooked' and when no soya is used 'white-cooked' – both are equally tasty. When all these ingredients are cooked together with a good quantity of vegetables, the result is usually very promising, especially with the addition of a little wine and sugar which help to enhance the richness of the dish.

Nonetheless, the Chinese seldom eat vegetables or vegetable dishes on their own. They exist in the context of a meal to complement the meat dishes on the one hand and the bulk cereal dishes on the other (i.e. rice, noodles or steamed buns). It takes the 'trinity' (meat, rice and vegetables) to make a complete Chinese meal. If, due to shortage, one of the components has to go, then the first to be dropped will be the meat dish because it is considered a 'luxury'. The next to be dropped if the squeeze is severe, will be the vegetables. Rice is the last bastion of the Chinese diet; this they must have if they are to exist, or at least the thin watery rice with shredded sweet potato or one of the other root vegetables added. That would be the 'last ditch'.

The vegetable dishes in this chapter are set out on their own rather than included in menus so that you can add any of these vegetable dishes to any of the menus in the earlier chapters. You can substitute them for a vegetable dish already in the menu or add them to a menu where there is a pronounced meat presence, either to increase the variety of dishes in a Chinese meal or to provide an additional dish because there is an extra mouth to be fed. In a Chinese meal, the extra dish or dishes are more likely to be vegetables than meat, if only because vegetables are more likely to be available than meats. It is also likely that it will be a semi-soup vegetable dish, which serves more than, say, a stir-fried dish.

The following is a dish which I frequently enjoyed while sitting on the lap of my grandmother, who was a practising Buddhist, over 65 years ago.

An ensemble of vegetables in consommé with noodles and dried mushrooms

(for 4 people with rice and 1 or 2 other dishes)

Preparation: 25 minutes   Cooking: 35 minutes

---

6 medium Chinese dried
  mushrooms
2 tablespoons dried shrimps
4–5 oz (100–150 g) bamboo-
  shoots
4–5 oz (100–150 g) asparagus
4–5 oz (100–150 g) broccoli
  stems
4–5 oz (100–150 g) cauliflower
  stems

3 oz (75 g) Chinese
  transparent pea-starch
  noodles
2 pints (1.2 litres) good stock
3 slices root ginger
1 chicken stock cube
salt and pepper to taste
1½ tablespoons light soya
  sauce
1½ teaspoons sesame oil

Preparation. Soak the dried mushrooms and dried shrimps for 20 minutes in a small bowl of hot water. Discard the mushroom stems and cut the caps into quarters. Cut the bamboo-shoots into 1½ × 2 inch (4 × 5 cm) triangular pieces. Cut the thinner parts of the vegetables into smaller natural shaped pieces. Remove the tough ends from the asparagus stalks and cut the remaining lengths into two.

Further cut the green spears and the white of the stalk slant-wise each into 2 or 3 pieces. Parboil the bamboo-shoots, broccoli, cauliflower and the white pieces of asparagus in boiling water for 2 minutes and drain. Soak the noodles in warm water for 2 minutes. Cut them with a pair of scissors, in the water, into 3 inch (7.5 cm) lengths and drain.

Cooking. Boil the stock in a saucepan or casserole. Add the ginger, dried shrimps, dried mushrooms, bamboo-shoots and the white parts of the asparagus. Bring to the boil, reduce the heat to low and simmer gently for 15 minutes. Add the broccoli, cauliflower, asparagus tips and crumbled stock cube. Bring to the boil, reduce the heat and simmer gently for 10 minutes. Add the noodles and adjust the seasoning with salt and pepper. Cook gently for a further 5 minutes. Sprinkle with soya sauce and sesame oil and serve.

Serving. Serve in a very large soup bowl or in the same casserole that has been used for cooking. The diners should help themselves by spooning the vegetables and liquid onto their rice in their own rice bowls and half eat and half drink the mixture along with the rice and other dishes provided. The rich vegetable flavour is very apparent in the dish, if only because of the quantity of its presence. Because of the length of cooking the vegetable pieces are, although tender, still somewhat crunchy in parts and they make an excellent complement to spicy meat dishes and the bland flavour of rice.

Stir-fry of noodles with vegetables and pickles
(for 4 people with rice and 1 or 2 other dishes)

Preparation: 30 minutes   Cooking: 15 minutes

In Chinese cooking one seldom uses one type of carbo-hydrate dish to complement another (e.g. noodles to comp-lement rice). Pea-starch noodles are perhaps the one excep-tion, probably because they are not made from ordinary rice or wheat starch, but from ground dried peas. They have the unusual quality of being able to withstand lengthy cooking without disintegrating or going entirely soft and mushy. They are also able to absorb an unusual amount of sauce or soup which makes them exceptionally good when cooked with meat or savoury sauces: such dishes are the great loves of the connoisseurs of Chinese home-cooking.

2 tablespoons dried shrimps
6 medium Chinese dried
  mushrooms
6 large button mushrooms
3 oz (75 g) bamboo-shoots
1 medium onion
3 spring onions
6 oz (175 g) French beans
2 oz (50 g) Chinese green
  'snow pickles' (or gherkins)

5 oz (150 g) transparent pea-
  starch noodles
3–4 rashers bacon
4½ tablespoons vegetable oil
2 oz (50 g) butter
2½ tablespoons light soya
  sauce
2 teaspoons Chinese shrimp
  sauce (optional)
2 teaspoons sesame oil

Preparation. Soak the dried shrimps and dried mushrooms in ¼ pint (150 ml) of boiling water for 30 minutes. Drain them and retain the water. Discard the mushroom stems and cut the caps into matchstick shreds. Cut the button mushrooms similarly, including the stems, having washed them well. Cut the bamboo-shoots into double matchstick shreds. Thinly slice the onion and spring onion into 2 inch (5 cm) lengths. Top and tail the French beans, parboil them for 3 minutes and drain. Coarsely chop the pickles or gherkins. Soak the noodles for 5 minutes in ample warm water, then cut them in the water with a pair of scissors into approximately 3 inch (7.5 cm) lengths and drain. Cut the bacon into shreds.

Cooking. Heat the oil in a large frying pan. Add the onion, dried mushrooms, shrimps and bacon and stir over medium heat for 2 minutes. Add the pickles, French beans and bamboo-shoots and stir-fry for 4 minutes. Stir in the noodles. Add the butter, fresh mushrooms and the mushroom/shrimp water, then sprinkle on the soya sauce and shrimp

169

sauce. Mix all the ingredients together evenly. Reduce the heat and allow to cool gently for 5 minutes, then sprinkle with spring onion and sesame oil.

Serving. When served with plain boiled rice, a vegetable and a meat dish, this should satisfy a good number of hungry mouths.

Stir-fried spinach with minced meat and bean curd

(For 4 people, with rice and 1 other dish, or served to augment an existing rice and 2-dish meal)

Preparation: 10 minutes   Soaking: 20 minutes
Cooking: 10 minutes

---

1 tablespoon dried shrimps	1½ teaspoons salt
4 medium Chinese dried mushrooms	¼ pint (150 ml) good stock
2 chillis	2½ tablespoons soya sauce
¾ lb (350 g) spinach	1½ tablespoons hoisin sauce (optional)
2 cakes bean curd	½ oz (15 g) butter
2 cloves garlic	½ chicken stock cube
4 tablespoons vegetable oil	pepper to taste
¼ lb (100 g) minced beef or pork	

Preparation. Soak the dried shrimps and mushrooms in a bowl of boiling water for 20 minutes. Discard the mushroom stems and coarsely chop the caps. Halve the chillis, remove the seeds and coarsely chop the flesh. Wash the spinach thoroughly, having removed any discoloured leaves and tougher stalks. Roll the leaves into a bunch and slice through with a knife at 2 inch (5 cm) intervals. Cut the bean curd into 1 inch (2.5 cm) cubes. Crush the garlic.

Cooking. Heat the oil in a casserole or large frying pan. Add the garlic, peppers, mushrooms, shrimps and stir-fry for 1 minute over high heat. Add the minced meat and salt

170

and stir-fry for 3 minutes. Add half the stock, soya sauce, hoisin sauce and continue to stir together for 3 minutes. Reduce the heat to low and leave to cook for 5 minutes. Remove the contents and put aside.

Melt the butter in the pan or casserole and add the spinach. Cook, turning frequently, until it is reduced to a third of its original volume. Pour in the remaining stock and sprinkle with crumbled stock cube. Add the bean curds and sprinkle with the remaining soya sauce and hoisin sauce. Turn them lightly with the spinach in the bubbling sauce, without mashing the bean curds. Return the minced meat to the pan and toss together lightly over medium heat for 3 minutes. Adjust the seasoning with salt and pepper.

Serving. This is a spicy dish, which is also highly nutritious. It should be served in a large bowl or deep dish for the diners to help themselves.

Spinach and radish salad

Preparation: 8 minutes   Seasoning: 30 minutes

10 large radishes	2 teaspoons caster sugar
5 teaspoons salt	pepper to taste
1 lb (450 g) spinach	1½ tablespoons vegetable oil
¼ chicken stock cube	1½ teaspoons sesame oil
1½ tablespoons good stock	

Preparation. Wash the radishes, then give each one a bash or two with the side of a heavy cleaver until it has cracked open all round. Place in a bowl and sprinkle with ¾ of the salt. Leave to season for 30 minutes. Remove the discoloured leaves and tougher stalks from the spinach. Blanch the spinach in boiling water for 30 seconds and drain. Squeeze out as much of the water as you can from the spinach. Place it on a chopping board and chop it through at regular ¼ inch (5 mm) intervals and then again at right angles to it at similar intervals. Loosen the spinach by turning and tossing with a fork. Dissolve the stock cube thoroughly in the stock, then sprinkle over the spinach, followed by the remaining salt, caster sugar, pepper, oil and sesame oil. Toss together until evenly seasoned.

Serving. Spread the spinach on a flat serving dish. Rinse the radishes quickly under running water. Drain and dry, then arrange on top of the spinach. The two vegetables together make a very colourful combination.

The Province of Szechuan (or Sichuan) is well known for its hot spicy food. Among its vegetable dishes there is a famous series of 'Boiled in the Water' recipes which are particularly suitable for eating with spicy, meaty dishes. The following 3 recipes are good examples of this style of cooking.

'Boiled in the water' Chinese white cabbage with watercress

Preparation: 5 minutes   Cooking: 5 minutes

¼ lb (100 g) watercress
1 small Chinese cabbage
   (about 1½–2 lbs (750 g–1
   kg))

½ pint (300 ml) good stock
½ chicken stock cube
salt and pepper to taste

Preparation. Wash the watercress thoroughly, trim and cut across at ½ in (1 cm) intervals. Wash the cabbage thoroughly, cut off the root end and break into individual leaves. Cut or tear the leaves into halves or quarters.

Cooking. Bring a large pan of water to the boil, add the cabbage and boil gently for 2 minutes. Add the watercress and continue gentle cooking for another ½ minute. Drain thoroughly. Bring the stock to the boil in a small saucepan, add the crumbled stock cube and dissolve well in the stock. Adjust the seasoning with salt and pepper to taste. Spread the cabbage and watercress evenly over the bottom of a large deep serving dish. Pour the boiling stock over them.

Serving. After 1 minute, serve by bringing the dish with the vegetables steaming in the clear consommé to the table. The purity of the dish contrasts well with any spicy or meaty dish.

'Boiled in the water' broccoli with cauliflower

Preparation: 5 minutes   Cooking: 7 minutes

1 lb (450 g) broccoli
1 lb (450 g) cauliflower
½ pint (300 ml) good stock
½ chicken stock cube

Preparation. Remove the stems of the vegetables. Break the broccoli into 1½–2 inch (4–5 cm) pieces, and the cauliflower into individual florets. Heat the stock in a small saucepan and add the crumbled stock cube.

Cooking. Plunge the cauliflower and broccoli into a large pan of boiling water to boil gently for 4 minutes. Drain thoroughly, then arrange in a large bowl or deep dish. Bring the stock in the saucepan to a high boil and pour it over the vegetables.

Serving. After 1 minute bring the bowl containing the steaming vegetables to the table. This is always an excellent complement to any rich stir-fried or 'red-cooked' dishes, eaten with rice.

'Boiled in the water' lettuce with mushrooms

Preparation: 5 minutes   Cooking: 5 minutes

1 Cos lettuce (about 1 lb
  (450 g))
¾ lb (350 g) firm button
  mushrooms

½ pint (300 ml) good stock
½ chicken stock cube

Preparation. Wash the lettuce and mushrooms thoroughly. Remove the stems from the mushrooms, cut the larger ones in half. Cut off the root end of the lettuce and cut the leaves horizontally at 2 inch (5 cm) intervals. Bring the stock to the boil and dissolve the crumbled stock cube in it.

Cooking. Cook the mushrooms in a large pan of boiling water for 2 minutes, add the lettuce and boil for 1 minute. Drain thoroughly.

Serving. Arrange the vegetables in a large bowl or deep serving dish. Bring the stock to a high boil and pour it over the vegetables. Bring the dish steaming to the table. Like the 2 previous dishes, these vegetables are excellent to complement any rich stir-fried or 'red-cooked' dishes and plain-cooked rice.

Hot-tossed courgettes with cauliflower and button mushrooms

Preparation: 10 minutes   Cooking: 10 minutes

2–3 medium courgettes
¼ lb (100 g) button
  mushrooms
1 medium cauliflower
1½ tablespoons dried shrimps

2 tablespoons vegetable oil
5 tablespoons chicken stock
1 tablespoon light soya sauce
½ chicken stock cube

Preparation. Clean the courgettes and cut into ⅛ inch (3 mm) slices. Cut the mushrooms through the stalks into quarters. Cut away the root and stem of the cauliflower and break into individual florets. Soak the dried shrimps in 4 tablespoons boiling water for 10 minutes, drain and reserve the water.

Cooking. Heat the oil in a frying pan with a lid. Add the vegetables and shrimps. Stir and mix together for 1½ minutes. Add the stock, soya sauce, shrimp water and sprinkle with the crumbled stock cube. Bring to the boil, stir and turn for 1½ minutes. Reduce the heat to low, cover tightly and leave to cook gently for 5–6 minutes.

Serving. Stir well and transfer to a serving dish.

The steamed marrow bowl

Preparation: 20 minutes   Cooking: 1 hour

This is more of a decorative party dish than an item for a quick home-cooked meal. Its contents can be varied according to available ingredients. When I last had it in China, in a banquet in Canton, the soup in the 'marrow bowl' was cooked from frogs' legs, while the marrow skin was carved as if it were made of ivory. But one need not go to such lengths and a presentable 'marrow bowl' can be prepared quite simply as in the following recipe. It is one of the semi-soups, which are excellent for serving with rice and a meat dish (i.e. as an addition to one of the menus in this book, where an extra dish would make it possible to feed another mouth or two.) For use as a 'bowl', the marrow will have to be reasonably large and squat.

1 tablespoon dried shrimps
4 large dried Chinese
  mushrooms
2 oz (50 g) ham or gammon
3½ oz (90 g) chicken breast
  meat
1¼ pints (750 ml) good stock
1 chicken stock cube

1 large marrow (at least 9
  inches (23 cm) in diameter
  and 1 ft (30 cm) long)
2 tablespoons green peas
1 small can Chinese straw
  mushrooms (or French
  champignon)
salt and pepper to taste

Preparation and cooking. Soak the dried shrimps and dried mushrooms in boiling water for 20 minutes. Drain, remove the mushroom stems and cut the caps into matchstick shreds. Dice the ham or gammon and chicken meat into cubes about the size of sugar lumps. Heat the stock in a saucepan, add the shrimps, ham, dried mushrooms and crumbled stock cube and simmer for 15 minutes. Meanwhile, cut the top quarter of the marrow off in one slice (retain the top slice for use later as 'lid' to the 'bowl'). Remove the flesh from inside the marrow, first with a knife and later with a spoon, leaving a shell ½ inch (1 cm) thick. Cut the excavated marrow pieces into regular sizes (discard the irregular pieces, as there will be more than enough).

Add the chicken, ham, peas, drained canned mushrooms and diced marrow to the stock. Bring to the boil, reduce the heat and cook gently for 10 minutes. Adjust the seasoning with salt and pepper. Pour the contents of the saucepan gently into the cavity of the excavated marrow. Close the top of the marrow with the sliced off 'lid', securing with a couple of toothpicks. Steady the marrow by standing it in a heatproof bowl and place in a steamer to steam for 30 minutes.

Serving. Bring the marrow mounted in the bowl to the dining table. Open the 'lid' by removing the toothpicks. A small ladle will be needed to spoon out the contents, which should not be eaten at once, as with Western soup, but in stages during the meal.

DESSERTS

Most Westerners interested in Chinese food must have gained the impression that we Chinese do not go in much for sweets. This is only partly true, and must be due to the fact that most Chinese restaurants do not serve many kinds of sweets. The chefs in Chinese restaurants are all primarily savoury cooks, who do not consider sweets and desserts as part of their business. They feel that people who are interested in these 'light-weight' foods should go to the confectioner's shop and not to a restaurant which deals only in savoury foods. Not being users of cream and dairy products, the Chinese have had to devise sweets and desserts quite independently of other cuisines. Because of the Chinese interest in their immense savoury repertoire, I think it is true to say that their interest in sweets and desserts is only cursory. This is another aspect of Chinese cooking which is healthy as everyone knows that sugar and cream are bad for you.

Anyone who has visited the Tung An Market (now called the East Wind Market) in Peking (Beijing) must have been impressed by the immense and colourful display of fresh and glacé fruits and dried preserved fruits (and nowadays canned fruits also). After all, fruits grow in profusion in China and they are frequently eaten at the dining table at the end of a meal. When prepared and served hot, as 'course breakers' they are often eaten during a multi-course party dinner. For instance, there are many Chinese 'fruit soups' and the 'Eight Treasure Rice' which is often served at dinner parties, is very much like a Christmas pudding with many nuts, dried and glacé fruits embedded in sweet, glutinous rice. But as this is a very heavy dessert and not very conducive to health, least

177

of all at the end of a heavy meal, I have not included a recipe for it in this book. When the Chinese require stuffings for sweet rice cakes, steamed buns or sweet multi-layer puddings, we usually use ground ingredients such as crab apples, dates, figs, lotus nuts, sweetened bean paste and sesame seeds.

However, in this book we shall confine ourselves to desserts which are healthy and easy to produce. These centre around fruits, 'fruit soups', 'fruit punches', sweet 'fruit congees'. Here are a few of them.

The Peking ice mountain fruit salad (for 4 to 5 people)

Preparation: 20 minutes

---

2 medium apples
2 medium pears
2 large peaches
2 × 1½ inch (4 cm) slices of melon
2 × 2 inch (5 cm) slices of pineapple

3 medium kiwi fruit
8 large black grapes
8 medium strawberries
3–4 lbs (1.25–1.75 kg) crushed ice

The difference between a Peking fruit salad and its average Western counterpart is that the fruits in a Chinese fruit salad are cut to about 3–4 times the size of fruits in a Western salad. This is because they are normally picked up with a pair of chopsticks and dipped into a dish of granulated or caster sugar before eating. You may be surprised that strawberries are used in the recipe, but they can be found growing in the countryside around Peking during the early summer. Although not a common fruit, they are in season when this fruit salad is commonly served.

Preparation. Peel the apples, cut a slice off the top and bottom and cut into 4–5 pieces. Do the same with the pears. Remove the stones from the peaches and cut each one into 4 pieces. Remove the skin and seeds from the melon and cut into large bite-sized pieces and cut the pineapple into similar pieces. Peel the kiwi fruit and cut each one in half. Wash the grapes and hull the strawberries.

Serving. Arrange the crushed ice as a bed in a large, deep dish. Build the ice into a slight mound in the centre and arrange the fruits on top and around it. Chill for 30 minutes to 1 hour. To serve, fill 2 saucer-sized dishes with sugar (caster or granulated) and place them beside the 'fruit mountain', to dip the fruits in before eating. For the diners to use their chopsticks to pick up one piece of fruit at a time and to eat it at a leisurely pace seems to be a much more elegant way of serving and eating fruit salad than the conventional way of using a spoon and treating it like porridge!

Sweet lotus nut soup (for 6 people)

Preparation: 10 minutes   Cooking: 15 minutes

The selection of fruits in this recipe can be the same as in the previous recipe, replacing the kiwi fruit and grapes with an 8 oz (225 g) can of mandarin oranges and 2 similar sized cans of lotus nuts. Cut the fruit into pieces twice as small as in the previous recipe. Dissolve 3 tablespoons sugar in 2 pints (1.2 litres) water and simmer the fruits in the syrup for 15 minutes. Blend 3 tablespoons cornflour with 6 tablespoons water and stir in to thicken the syrup.

Serving. Serve in a large soup bowl, or a glass bowl which will show the colours of the different fruits, for the diners to help themselves. The mild sweetness of the 'soup' has a settling effect on the stomach after consuming a quantity of savoury food, and the nuttiness of the lotus provides an added interest.

Sweet congee with a selection of fruits *(for 6 people)*

Preparation: 10 minutes   Cooking: 15 minutes

Here the same selection and quantity of fruits as in the previous recipes are cooked for 15 minutes in 2 pints (1.2 litres) of prepared congee (soft watery rice) (page 114). Add a large dollop of brown sugar to the middle of each bowl, for the diners to mix gradually into the 'soup' as they proceed to consume it. In the winter a large bowl of this sweet 'fruit congee' can have a very warming and comforting effect. A large dollop of sweet bean-paste (when available) may also be added to the congee together with the brown sugar.

Sweet orange and cherry 'tea' *(for 6 people)*

Preparation: 10 minutes   Cooking: 15 minutes

These 'sweet teas' which are lighter than sweet 'soups' or 'congees' are used in China more as 'course breakers' in the context of a multi-dish banquet or party meal, whereas the soups or congees are desserts which usually conclude a meal. The teas are simple to prepare and are mostly served between two series of main courses.

To make sweet orange tea, heat 1¾ pints (1 litre) of water in a saucepan. Add 1½ tablespoons sugar and ¼ pint (150 ml) of freshly squeezed orange juice, 2–3 medium mandarin oranges (peeled and chopped into small pieces) and 12 red cherries (fresh or canned) and simmer for 10 minutes.

This clear, sparkling soup, which is mildly sweet and slightly sharp (due to the chopped oranges), is very refreshing and acts as a cleanser to the palate in the steady progression of numerous dishes of a multi-course Chinese banquet.

Sweet almond 'tea' *(for 6 people)*

Preparation: 5 minutes   Cooking: 10 minutes

In contrast to the previous recipe, which is a clear 'soup', this is a thick 'soup' which is used more often to conclude a meal, and not as a 'course-breaker'.

1½ pints (900 ml) water
6 tablespoons ground almonds
4 tablespoons rice flour
4 tablespoons sugar

1 small can (5 fl oz) (150 ml)
  evaporated milk
1 teaspoon almond essence

Preparation and cooking. Heat the water in a heavy saucepan. When it boils add the ground almonds, rice flour and sugar. Stir until the contents reboil. Reduce the heat to very low and put an asbestos sheet under the pan. Stir and cook very gently for 10 minutes. Stir in the evaporated milk and almond essence. When the contents reboil, stir to blend evenly and the 'tea' should be ready.

Serving. The introduction of a nutty taste into sweets is a Chinese speciality. This 'almond tea' is extremely hot when freshly cooked and should be allowed to cool a little before being sipped from small bowls.

Almond junket with fruit salad *(for 6 people)*

Preparation: 10 minutes   Cooking: 10 minutes
Cooling: 1½–2 hours

¾ pint (450 ml) water
2 sachets gelatine
4 tablespoons ground almonds
4 tablespoons sugar

1 teaspoon almond essence
1 small can (5 fl oz (150 ml))
  evaporated milk

Preparation. Heat ⅓ of the water in a small pan. Stir in the gelatine to dissolve thoroughly. Heat the remaining water in another saucepan. Add the ground almonds blended

181

with the melted gelatine and the sugar. Stir until boiling, then reduce the heat to low and continue to stir and cook gently for 5–6 minutes. Add the almond essence and evaporated milk and stir until thoroughly blended. Continue stirring for 2–3 minutes, then remove the pan from the heat. When cool, pour the mixture into a square dish and chill for 2 hours.

Serving. When the mixture has set firmly, cut it into 1¼ inch (3 cm) triangular shaped pieces and serve them in a conventional Western fruit salad instead of cream, or in addition to cream. The nutty taste of the pieces of 'junket' adds a new element of interest to the fruit salad.

Sweet rice-cake stuffed with sweet bean paste or ground dates *(for 6 people)*

Preparation: 30 minutes   Cooking: 8 minutes

¾ lb (350 g) short-grain rice
2 tablespoons butter or lard

6 tablespoons ground dates or sweet bean-paste
6–8 tablespoons vegetable oil

Preparation. Wash the rice, then simmer in 1½ times its volume of water. Turn the heat off, cover and allow the rice to cook in the residual heat for 10 minutes. Add the butter (or lard) and stir it evenly into the rice. When cool, form the rice into a long strip and cut into 12 pieces. Form each piece into a flat round cake. Place ½ tablespoon bean paste or ground dates in the centre of each of the cakes and fold in half. Reform the cakes.

Cooking. Heat the oil in a large heavy frying pan tilting the pan so the surface is evenly greased. Place the round cakes, one at a time, well spread out in the pan. Fry them gently for 1½ minutes on each side. Turn over with a fish slice and fry for a further 2 minutes on each side, or until lightly brown.

Serving. Serve as hot cakes. With a crisp outside, and sweetness of dates inside, sandwiched by sweet stickiness of the glutinous rice, these cakes are by no means unattractive to the Western palate. There are numerous cakes of this type in China, usually served at festival times and not necessarily during a meal. They are not particularly healthy, but the children love them and they are no worse than chocolates as an indulgence.

Steamed pears in honeyed syrup *(for 4 people)*

Preparation: 8 minutes   Cooking: 30 minutes
Chilling: 1 hour

4 medium pears
8 tablespoons boiling water
4 tablespoons sugar
4 tablespoons honey

6 tablespoons cherry brandy, crème de menthe or Chinese 'rose dew'

Preparation. Choose unblemished pears. Peel them carefully, leaving the stem and about ¼ inch (5 mm) of the surrounding skin intact for ease of handling.

Cooking. Stand the pears in a deep heatproof dish. Pour half a kettle of boiling water over them. Pour half the water away, then put the dish with the pears into a steamer and steam vigorously for 20–30 minutes (depending upon hardness). Meanwhile, while the pears are steaming, dissolve the sugar in the boiling water and stir in the honey. Stir continuously until all the solids have dissolved. Add the liqueur and stir until well blended.

Serving. Divide the pears between small individual bowls. Pour the sauce evenly over them covering the peeled surface of each pear. Chill for at least 1 hour before serving.

GLOSSARY

Bean Curd (Toufu). Ground soya beans which have been lightly cooked with water and then left to set into a semi-solid 'custard'. This is cut into cakes approximately 2 inches (5 cm) square. Because of its high protein content, bean curd is an important ingredient in Chinese cooking and is widely used.

Black Bean Sauce (see also Soya Paste). Small, black, salted soya beans which are soaked in water and then ground into a paste. Soya Paste is another name for it.

Chilli Sauce (and Chilli Oil). Chilli sauce is a hot sauce made from small chilli peppers. Chilli oil, which is even hotter, is made from small, red, chilli peppers which are slowly fried in oil. The oil becomes coloured by the peppers in the process of being heated, and the chilli oil, when ready for use, is reddish in colour.

Chinese Cabbage. A firm lettuce-like plant with long, crisp leaves. It can be braised, stir-fried or made into a salad and is very tasty.

Chinese Dried Mushrooms. These are dark brown in colour, and must be soaked for about 30 minutes before use. The stem should be removed altogether as it is very tough. Dried mushrooms have a much stronger flavour than fresh mushrooms, and have a meatier texture. They are used more in Chinese cooking than fresh mushrooms.

Chinese Noodles. There are three types of Chinese noodles – wheat-flour, rice-flour and pea-starch transparent noodles. The first two are used as accompaniments to vegetables, meat and fish, while the pea-starch noodles are often used in soups as they absorb a lot of liquid while cooking and become very flavoursome.

Chinese 'Snow' Pickle and 'Winter' Pickle. 'Snow' pickle is made from salted, mustard greens in vinegar and it comes in cans. 'Winter' pickle is made from thinly shredded dried, salted turnips and is sold in earthenware jars. Both these pickles are used mainly for flavouring meat, fish and vegetable dishes and are not normally eaten on their own.

Congee Rice. 'Congee' is a Chinese word meaning rice-porridge, or watery rice. It must be cooked for a long time in at least five times its own weight of water and is often served for breakfast in China.

Dried Shrimps. Dried shrimps need soaking for about 20 minutes before using. They are one of the most widely used Chinese flavouring agents and are often used in soups, or fried with other ingredients to add flavour to savoury dishes.

Five Spice Powder. Consists of five types of ground, dried spices: star anise, anise pepper, fennel, cloves and cinnamon.

Hoisin Sauce. Literally translated this means 'sea-fresh sauce'. It is made from soya sauce, soya paste, ground yellow beans, garlic pulp, sugar and vinegar. Sweet and spicy, it is often combined with other sauces for use as a dip and is also used in the cooking of seafood, meat and vegetables.

Lotus Nuts. These are the seeds of the lotus flower and are used for making sweet soups and as fillings for sweet dumplings. They can be bought canned.

Oyster Sauce. A rich sauce made from oysters, oyster water and soya sauce. It is used to flavour seafood, meat, poultry and vegetable dishes.

Pea-starch Transparent Noodles (described under Chinese Noodles).

Rice-flour Noodles (described under Chinese Noodles).

Root Ginger. This is ginger in its raw state which is usually thinly sliced, chopped or minced. It is used extensively in Chinese cooking in the preparation of many fish and meat dishes.

Salted Turnips. These are turnips in their natural state but salted. The Chinese often eat them for breakfast.

Sesame Oil. This is the oil produced from sesame seeds. It has a strong, nutty flavour and is used sparingly for flavouring.

Shrimp Sauce. This bottled sauce is used to add flavour to soups, noodles, vegetables, and meat dishes Surprisingly, it is not used for flavouring fish dishes.

Sichuan Pepper. These peppers are grown in Sichuan and are brownish-red in colour. They are sometimes used whole or ground with a pestle.

Soya Paste (see also Black Bean Sauce). This can almost be described as a solid version of soya sauce. It is a thick sauce made from ground, salted soya beans. It can be made from either black or yellow soya beans and it is very salty. Soya paste can be used in conjunction with soya sauce but should be used sparingly.

Soya Sauce (dark or light). Dark soya sauce is used with meat and light soya sauce with vegetables, fish dishes and in soups. Soya sauce is strong in flavour and used extensively in Chinese cooking. Both kinds are sold in bottles.

Star Anise. A dark brown, star-shaped seed, called 'eight point' in China, used as a flavouring ingredient. It has a very distinctive flavour of aniseed.

Sweet Potato. Sweet potatoes are four or five times the size of ordinary potatoes and slightly sweet in flavour. They are eaten boiled or steamed and often used as a supplement to rice as a bulk food. They feature quite a lot in Caribbean and Mexican cooking.

Sweet Red Bean Paste. This is made from ground red beans that have been sweetened. It is used for filling sweet dumplings and for making Eight Precious Rice Pudding, which is almost a kind of Chinese Christmas Pudding.

Tangerine Peel. The dried skin of tangerines used for flavouring duck and red-simmered dishes.

INDEX